THE MUDSKIPPER

Ovidia Yu is based in Singapore. She is an award-winning novelist, short-story writer and playwright. Her plays have been peformed locally and abroad. This book was one of the winners of the Scholastic Asian Book Award 2011.

To all at NBDCS and Scholastic Asia who organised the SABA competition, with thanks

Published by Scholastic India Pvt. Ltd.
A subsidiary of Scholastic Inc., New York, 10012 (USA).
Publishers since 1920, with international operations in Canada, Australia, New Zealand, the United Kingdom, India, and Hong Kong.

For information regarding permission, write to:
Scholastic India Pvt. Ltd.
A-27, Ground Floor, Sigma Centre
Infocity-1, Sector 34, Gurgaon 122001 (India)

First edition: April 2012
Reprint: November 2014, January 2018

ISBN-13: 978-81-8477-852-6

Printed at Shivam Offset Press, New Delhi

The Lexile measure of this book (870L) represents the complexity of the text. This Lexile measure—along with other characteristics of the text, such as developmental level and subject matter—helps in selecting books that best match a reader's level and goals. For more information on using Lexile measures to connect readers with text, visit www.Lexile.com.

THE MUDSKIPPER

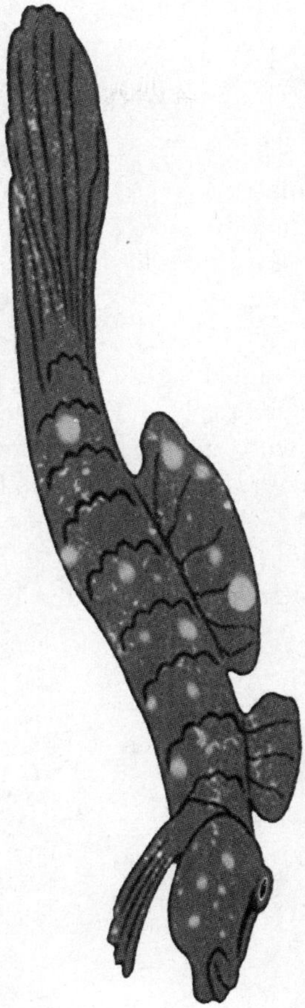

Ovidia Yu

Illustrations by Sanket Pethkar

SCHOLASTIC
New York Toronto London Auckland
Sydney New Delhi Hong Kong

IN A TAXI IN SINGAPORE

The taxi carrying Lizhi and her mother stopped outside the gate to a big house. There was a fence around the garden and in the early morning light it looked like there were parts of it falling off that had been patched back with bits of rope. Even from inside the car Lizhi could see the garden was full of trees and plants and long grass. That made her happy. She liked trees.

'Are you sure this is the right place?' her mother asked. She did not seem as happy as Lizhi to see all the plants and grass and trees.

'This is the address you asked for,' said the taxi driver. 'Neo Tiew Crescent you said, right?'

'I suppose this is the house then,' Lizhi's mother said, with a small sigh.

'What does Neo Tiew mean?' Lizhi asked again. She had already asked once at the start of the journey but neither of the grown-ups had replied.

When Lizhi and her mother had landed at the Singapore airport it was already so late that the night was turning into morning. The airport was very big and bright and grand and clean, and there were plants and even ponds with fish inside the building. Even though Lizhi was tired she would have liked to explore, but her mother said, 'We should go straight out—just in case someone is waiting for us. I told them what flight we were coming on and I didn't get an answer before we left.'

'It's beautiful here,' Lizhi said. 'But Singapore is much colder than France!'

Lizhi's mother laughed. 'That's because of the air-conditioning,' she said. 'Outside it will be much much warmer!'

And so it was. Although it was still dark outside the airport terminal it was already warm. There were many people holding up signs and notices to welcome the new arrivals but there was no one waiting to meet them.

'I didn't really expect anyone to come,' Lizhi's mother said as they walked to the taxi queue. 'Your grandfather is an old man and not in the best of health. And your Aunt Mona has to look after him.'

'Aunt Mona is Papa's sister, isn't she?' Of course Lizhi knew who she was. She had heard so many family stories from her father, but she just wanted to run through it all again, the way she revised her lessons before a test. After all, this was the first time she was meeting these relations her father had told her so much about since she was little, and she wanted to make a good first impression. Lizhi's father used to say it was important to make a good first impression because once people got the wrong impression it was very difficult to make them change their minds.

Anyone who had known him would have thought it funny that he believed that because he had never paid much attention to how he looked. Lizhi's mother used to say it drove her crazy trying to make sure he didn't have paint on his clothes or hair when he was going for an appointment. But the physical appearance—with or without paint—was not the sort of impression that had mattered to her father.

'And it was Aunt Mona who helped Papa get away to marry you, wasn't it? And she warned Papa and you about how angry Grandfather was. And she used to be a teacher. Do you think Aunt Mona will teach me my lessons like Papa used to?'

Lizhi's mother smiled at her. 'I think you deserve a little holiday,' she said. 'Your Papa believed that as long as you learn to read and write that's all you really need to know. But if you ever want a job working with other people, you need to pass exams, to show them that you can fit in and do the work. Anyway, you may be going to school soon so you'll be getting all the lessons you want then.'

'To school?' Lizhi was amazed and delighted. Because her family had travelled so much she had never attended school regularly like most children did. The idea of having the same friends to play with every day, for weeks and months and perhaps even years, appealed to her tremendously.

'Oh that would be wonderful! But Papa said I would go to school when you decided where we were going to settle down. Does that mean you're going to settle down? Where?'

It probably hurt her mother to remember all the plans she had made with her husband, but she only ran her hand through her excited little daughter's hair and said, 'Look, I think we're almost there—'

It was hard to see where they were. The roads out of the

airport and through the city had all been brilliantly bright with the glowing streetlights and the lights inside the buildings. But they had been driving for a very long time now. There were expressways and highways and so many buildings that after a while they all started looking the same to Lizhi. Or perhaps that was only because she was very tired, even while the sky had been turning lighter and lighter grey and was now the pale blue of morning.

And then the taxi had turned off the expressway and onto smaller, darker roads that seemed to twist and turn. Lizhi had almost fallen asleep. After all, because of the time difference, her insides still felt as though it was the middle of the night. But now she was awake and excited. The house was big—much bigger than Lizhi had expected—and raised off the ground on square pillars so there was a space beneath it and people had to go upstairs to get to the front balcony. There were trees all around.

The taxi drew up at the gate and honked before Lizhi's mother could stop him.

'Maybe we should get out here—' she said. 'I need you to wait, if you don't mind. I'm just going to settle my daughter in, and then I have to go back to the airport to catch my flight out.'

'Aiyoh, you leaving the small girl here, ah?' the taxi driver asked. He shook his head. 'Are these people expecting you?'

'Yes, of course they are. I gave them the flight number and

the time of arrival ...'

'Then *lagi* they should open the gate,' the taxi driver said. 'I'm not going to carry her luggage from here into the house, and looking at you, I don't think you can.' He tooted his horn again.

Lizhi's mother looked worried but her daughter giggled. She liked the taxi driver. He talked the same way her father did when he was teasing her mother.

They saw a small figure walking down the long driveway from the house towards them.

'Maybe this isn't such a good idea after all,' Lizhi's mother said. She put her arm around Lizhi. 'Maybe this isn't such a good idea at all.'

IN THE NOT-SO-OLD DAYS

Looking at Lizhi Wang in the taxi you would see an excited girl with pale brown skin, big curious eyes and curly black hair. Even though she was almost ten years old, Lizhi had never met her grandfather or her Aunt Mona or any of her father's relatives before.

Years ago Michael Wang, Lizhi's father, had been born in Singapore. He had lived in Singapore all his life until he went to England to study. There he met another foreign student, Juliette Fournier, Lizhi's mother (though of course Lizhi was not born till much later) and they fell in love and got married ... and neither they nor Lizhi had been back to Singapore since.

Michael Wang had died last year so he would never go back to Singapore now. But right after the funeral service Lizhi's mother had said to her, 'We'll make a visit to Singapore to meet your Papa's family.'

'Why?' Lizhi had asked.

'Because I promised your father,' her mother had replied. 'Anyway, even if they don't want to see me it's about time they met you!'

Lizhi knew that her mother always did what she promised.

Juliette was also an artist like Lizhi's father had been, but instead of painting she wove cloth and knotted fabrics with beads and gold thread. People bought her materials for making dresses and bags and wall hangings. Juliette always said leaving just one loose thread could make everything unravel, so she always tied up loose ends, and to her, promises were loose ends until she had done what she had promised. It did not make any difference whether it was a promise she made to someone who wanted to buy one of her paintings or whether it was a promise to Lizhi to make her favourite avocado sandwiches; if Lizhi's mother made a promise she kept her word.

It had been very different with Michael Wang. Even though he had the best of intentions he had always been absentminded and forgetful, especially while painting. Juliette said that because painters could hide anything they didn't like with more paint, they were only concerned with what was on the surface.

'But what lies beneath will always be there,' Michael used to tell her. 'Even if you don't see it—the texture, the foundations are there.'

And even if he often forgot things, he had always kept his promises too—only not as promptly as Juliette.

So ever since her father's funeral Lizhi knew it was only a matter of time before they went to Singapore to visit his family. In fact, she was surprised it had taken them so long. Her father had died almost a year ago.

Lizhi was still not used to that. There were moments when she saw something special—like a colour in the sky or a bird flying or water shining and automatically she would look around for her father, to tell him to look, because she knew it would make him happy and excited … and then, with a sinking feeling, she would remember that he was dead and would never be there to look at things with her in their special way again.

It had happened so quickly and unexpectedly that as Lizhi heard her mother say to a friend, 'Right now, the shock is greater than the loss.'

Jeremiah, who had also been a great friend of her father's, said, 'The loss will be with us forever. We have a lifetime to deal with it. So just try to survive the shock now.'

It was a very great shock, especially for Juliette, who for years had worried that her husband would fall off a cliff or that a rock would fall on his head while he was up on a ladder painting walls and ceilings or out climbing trees and rock faces to collect samples and specimens so that he could paint them. When he was working he sometimes got so engrossed that he did not know what was happening around him. Juliette used to joke, 'When Michael is painting a tree he becomes a part of that tree!'

But he had not been working when he died. He had been hit by a car while on the pedestrian crossing. The car did not stop and Lizhi's father had gone to hospital and died three days later.

'It's no use getting angry,' Juliette said. 'It won't bring him back.'

Lizhi had been angry with the driver and angry with her father for being on the road where the driver could kill him. For a while she was even angry with her mother for being upset, as well as angry with her for not being more upset. That was the shock, Jeremiah told her. 'It's harder for your mother. Be strong for her, won't you? Please?'

And Lizhi had tried. As Jeremiah pointed out, her mother had known her father much longer than Lizhi had—so she would miss him even more.

Lizhi wanted more than anything to go back to the old days but it was of no use saying so. She tried not to think about her father because when she did it was impossible to do anything except sit down and cry and she didn't want to do that because when she cried her mother cried too. But though she did not tell her mother, Lizhi was also afraid of forgetting her father. At night after her mother had put her to bed, Lizhi would lie with her eyes shut and try to remember specific things about him. There were big memories like birthdays and celebrating new paintings and how he had loved birds and trees and fish … and there were small memories like when she saw her father standing outside the room waiting for her to finish her music lesson or Mandarin class. There were many small memories that ran into each other and it was difficult to untangle them. But Lizhi didn't want to forget any of it so she played them over and over again in her mind until she fell asleep.

Sometimes her mother brought up memories too. For example, during the flight out to Singapore, she said, 'Do you remember when your Papa tried to make soup inside a melon?

He tried to stuff it with mushrooms and onions because he wanted to paint an authentic Chinese meal—'

'—and then it fell apart and all over the floor when he tried to take it out of the oven!' Lizhi did remember.

It had been a disaster as a dish but they had enjoyed watching him. He insisted he had seen it done (or rather he had seen the result served to him on a dinner table). Anyway, he had finally made a model out of clay and photographed and painted that instead.

'We should look it up in Singapore,' Juliette said. 'Find a restaurant that serves melon soup and go and try it. Then we'll know what your Papa was trying to share with us.'

Lizhi liked the idea of getting to know the things that her father had liked in Singapore. Understanding some of the things he had talked about would be a way of getting to know him better even though he was gone.

'He also liked monkey bananas,' Lizhi remembered, 'and blocks of sweet corn and red bean ice cream that you eat out of a folded piece of bread, and mangosteens that are purple outside but white inside and have the same number of segments inside as the pattern on the outside.' Perhaps being in Singapore wouldn't be so bad after all.

But then her mother added quietly, 'And you can finally meet your father's relatives. It is about time.'

Even though Juliette did not say so, Lizhi could tell from her voice that her mother was not looking forward to this.

Juliette was French and Michael Wang was Singaporean. Even though Lizhi's parents had never discussed it with her, she knew that was part of the reason why her father's family was not happy that he had married her mother.

Lizhi's mother's great-grandparents had come to France from Cameroon in Africa. Her father's grandparents had come to Singapore from Canton in China. Cameroon and Canton were even further apart than France and Singapore were.

Listening to her parents talk, Lizhi knew there was another reason why they had never visited Singapore. Her Singaporean grandparents were also upset because they had wanted her father to be a doctor or a lawyer. This would have been for his own good because as a doctor or lawyer Michael Wang would have been able to earn enough to support a wife and children. Even though he wanted to be an artist, Michael would have become a doctor like his parents wanted if he had not met Juliette and fallen in love with her. Juliette told Michael she thought it was more important to work at something you really loved than to make a lot of money for children you might never have. That was why Lizhi's grandparents didn't like her mother.

Then after they were married, Lizhi was born. By then both Lizhi's parents were too happy being artists to ever want to do anything else. They travelled a lot because Michael loved painting in new places. He did not paint on canvases like most other artists. He painted on walls, usually the walls of buildings. People would fly him to different places and ask him to paint the insides and outsides of their houses and restaurants and banks and sometimes even museums. And when he was between painting jobs, he loved travelling around the world to get ideas for new paintings. Michael was most famous for painting scenes that critics said were a cross between fantasy and memory. But he himself always said he painted what made him happy.

Lizhi's parents took her with them wherever they went and she learned to eat what they were eating and would play with her colouring books while they were working, so having a child did not cost them too much money after all. At least it had worked for them right up to the time her father died. Though even before that they had sometimes talked about, 'When Lizhi has to go to a regular school—'.

Lizhi didn't think she needed to go to school. Her father taught her reading and maths and Mandarin and her mother taught her music and geography (depending on which country they were in at the time) and French. Lizhi knew that her mother had worried about it more than her father had, 'It's not just the lessons. Lizhi will have no trouble doing the lessons. But how will she get used to working around other people?'

That was the part Lizhi could not understand. She had never had any trouble getting along with any of the people she met.

'Don't you like Singapore?' Lizhi remembered asking her father when she was younger. He had looked surprised. 'Of course I like Singapore. Why do you say that?'

'Then why don't we ever visit your family in Singapore?' Lizhi saw her father look at her mother before answering.

'Do you want to visit Singapore? Do you want to visit your relatives there?'

Lizhi thought about it. 'Maybe one day,' she said.

'All right, we'll go to Singapore one day,' her father said.

THE MUDSKIPPER

While Juliette paid the taxi driver, Lizhi got out of the car and looked through the gate. This was the house that her father had grown up in. All her life (until he died last year) he had told her stories about growing up in Singapore. He had told her about this house and about how the garden behind it led right down to the sea where he had had his own boat. When it was high tide the boat floated on the water beyond the sea wall, he had said. And when it was low tide the bottom of the boat lay on the sand.

Her father had always said he would bring her for a visit one day when the time was right. Lizhi thought the problem with waiting for the right time was that the time could go from 'not yet' to 'too late' before you knew it. It was like cooking eggs in their shells when you couldn't see from the outside whether they were ready yet.

'Well, better late than never,' Juliette said as she got out of the taxi, as though she was thinking the same thing.

The taxi driver was thinking of something else altogether. 'I go *makan* first—later come back and get you,' he said to Juliette.

Lizhi's mother looked flustered, 'When will you come back?' she asked.

The taxi driver shrugged, 'How long you going to take?'

'I don't know—if you don't mind waiting just a while …'

Lizhi knew why her mother was looking worried. They were not just going to see her grandparents for the first time. Lizhi was supposed to stay with her grandfather and Aunt Mona while her mother went to China to talk to some people. These people wanted to buy her father's last paintings, but it was more complicated than just saying 'yes' because the way he had painted meant they had to buy the buildings he had painted on and take the walls apart then reassemble them. Her mother was going to talk to them about how this could be done and where they could put the painted walls.

'If they want your Papa's last paintings and will pay for them we won't have to worry about money for a long time,' Lizhi's mother told her. 'So this is very important. But I can't take you to China with me. You will be good, won't you?'

The small figure was still coming down the driveway towards them.

'Are there any children here?' Lizhi asked. 'Are there cousins my age to play with?'

'Children? Oh no. I don't think so. Your Aunt Mona said it's just her and your grandfather. And I think there is an old gardener. Your father used to talk about a poor old gardener who could not do much but they could not fire him because he had nowhere to go.'

Juliette looked sad. She always looked sad when she talked about her husband. But still she tried to talk to Lizhi about her father as often as possible because she said it was important for Lizhi to remember him.

'Sorry! Sorry!' It was a small dark girl who started to fumble with the chain holding the gate shut. 'I quickly, I quickly already!'

Lizhi watched her with some interest. It looked like there would be someone for her to play with after all. Or even if the girl didn't want to play with someone her age (as Lizhi knew older children sometimes did not) she might have books or toys that Lizhi could borrow. Because they had packed in such a hurry to come to Singapore, her mother had not let her bring anything other than clothes with her.

So there was at least another person in the house besides Lizhi's grandfather and Aunt Mona.

Lizhi knew her grandmother had died the year before her father's accident. He had been very upset about that, because his father had not let Aunt Mona write to tell him that his mother was dead until after the funeral. Then she wrote to say that her grandfather said there was no point in them coming to Singapore because the funeral was already over. Lizhi's father had been upset and angry with his father until Juliette had said, 'Do you want to teach your daughter to be angry with her father? Because that's the example you are setting, you know!'

Lizhi's father said that was totally different but still he stopped being so angry—at least he stopped being so angry out loud.

'I wanted my mum to see her granddaughter. Lizhi is her only grandchild,' Michael had been almost tearful. 'If anything could have made her accept us—'

'Being accepted by everybody is not always possible—or important,' Lizhi's mother had said.

When Michael died Juliette had sent a letter to Lizhi's grandfather, but he had not replied. Aunt Mona had sent a condolence card, but it was signed only by her. Apparently her grandfather was not the sort of man to forgive people what they had done while they were alive just because they were now dead.

'Come this way! Please madam!' the small dark girl who had opened the gate said to them. She was even skinnier than Lizhi, and though Lizhi was only ten years old they were almost the same height. Lizhi thought maybe they could be friends after all.

'What's your name?' Lizhi asked her. 'Do you live here? How old are you?'

But the girl just stood there holding the gate, saying, 'Please madam, come this way!'

The girl was waving at the taxi to go up the drive, so the taxi driver opened the back door of the taxi again (Lizhi liked how he could do that without touching the handle) and said, 'You might as well let me drive you in. After last night's rain it is sure to be muddy.'

It was a very long driveway, with long grass growing on both sides; in some places the grass almost covered the driveway. When they finally pulled up at the house they saw it was raised off the ground on short pillars, with steps leading up to a sheltered porch.

It was a very grand but very old house. Lizhi could see that because the paint on the walls was streaked with different colours from the rain and the sun. These were exactly the kind of walls that her father had loved to paint on the most.

A figure was standing at the top of the steps, watching them. It did not move as Juliette and the taxi driver lifted Lizhi's bags out of the boot and Juliette paid him and gave him some money for breakfast.

The taxi driver said he would find somewhere nearby to eat. He gave Juliette his mobile phone number. 'You call, ten minutes tops I come back here,' he said.

'Can I have a mobile phone?' Lizhi asked her mother.

'Not now, darling,' Juliette replied distractedly. She was trying to straighten her clothes and pick up Lizhi's bags and water bottle and smile at the figure standing on the porch all at the same time.

'Where is the girl who opened the gate? Is she my cousin?' Lizhi called up to the woman on the porch.

'The maid is waiting to lock up the gate after the taxi leaves,' the woman said coldly. Though she did not shout, she spoke loudly enough to be heard by the taxi driver who was telling Lizhi's mother through the window about the best places to eat in that part of Singapore. Both the taxi driver and Juliette looked guilty, and the taxi driver wound up his window and turned his car around.

Lizhi looked down the driveway, watched the taxi drive away and waited for the dark girl to show up, but she did not. She did see a brown and white cat walk slowly across the driveway with its tail straight up in the air. Lizhi liked cats. Perhaps it would not be so bad staying here for a few days after all.

AUNT MONA

Aunt Mona was Lizhi's father's elder and only sister. At least Lizhi assumed it was her Aunt Mona who was watching them, standing on the porch on top of the stairs. Looking at her, Lizhi saw a woman whose plump, square face had a fixed smile. Two dark eyes gleamed brightly.

'Hello, Juliette,' Aunt Mona said.

Aunt Mona sounded like Lizhi's mother did when she was cross.

Juliette seemed to think so too. She looked guilty and confused. The two women shook hands, then Aunt Mona looked at Lizhi and said, 'So this is the child? She's very dark, isn't she?'

'I'm not as dark as Mama,' Lizhi pointed out. 'And I'm not as fair as Papa. Papa said it's like when you mix watercolours—you end up with a colour that's in between. I'm the in between.'

Aunt Mona looked at Lizhi while she spoke but did not answer.

'Good to finally meet you, Mona. This is Lizhi,' Juliette said. 'Say hello to your Aunt Mona, Lizhi.'

'Hello, Aunt Mona,' Lizhi said properly, the way she had been taught. 'My name is Lizhi Wang. Pleased to meet you.'

Aunt Mona looked at Lizhi the same way Lizhi's mother might look at a dead bug.

'She doesn't look very Chinese,' Aunt Mona said. 'Why did you give her a Chinese name? It sounds so funny. People will think it's so funny.'

'Well, Michael thought that since she's part Chinese—'

Aunt Mona's face changed.

'And she's so skinny,' Aunt Mona said. 'Is she a picky eater? I can't stand girls who are picky eaters!'

Later Lizhi would realise Aunt Mona changed the subject every time her dead brother Michael's name was mentioned.

When she looked at Aunt Mona sideways or glanced very quickly at her, Lizhi could think for a moment that it was her father standing there, but it was as though she was seeing him through a magnifying glass. Aunt Mona was almost the same height as her father but she was at least twice as wide.

'Do I remind you of your father?' Aunt Mona asked Lizhi. Without waiting for her to answer Aunt Mona turned to her mother and continued, 'Look at the girl, look at the way she's staring at me! Well, people were always saying how alike we two looked, you know. All the time when we were growing up.'

'You don't look like my father,' Lizhi said to Aunt Mona.

Of course Aunt Mona's hair and her skin were the same colour as her father's had been, but Lizhi thought that was probably how Chinese people looked rather than how her father's family looked.

'Actually I was also hoping that Lizhi could get a chance to get to know you and her grandfather. You are the only other relatives she has and I know her father wanted her to get to know you and Singapore. Is your father home?' Aunt Mona's father was also Lizhi's grandfather.

'My father is resting in hospital. He's not well enough to see anybody. Lizhi can stay here until you get back from China.

When I'm at work the maid can keep an eye on her. I hope you are not going to be too long. Bwe Bwe! Come here!'

Bwe Bwe was the Indonesian maid who had unlocked the gate for them. She had come up to stand on the steps behind them so quietly that they had not realised she was there. Bwe Bwe was a small, dark girl not much taller than Lizhi.

'Hi,' Lizhi said to her. Bwe Bwe smiled shyly at her.

Aunt Mona went on talking to Lizhi's mother. 'The girl can stay here while the old man is in hospital. The timing is all for the best, really. He doesn't like having a lot of noisy children running around. Of course there's no question of disturbing him in hospital. His doctors would never allow it!'

'I'm just one child, not a lot of children,' Lizhi said. 'And I'm not noisy. I can be very quiet if you want me to be. And I know how to behave in hospitals.'

Lizhi knew all about hospitals because of those terrible days when her father was in hospital dying.

'My father doesn't want to see you,' Aunt Mona said. 'He won't change his mind. He asked me to find out the real reason why you brought the girl all the way here. The girl's very dark isn't she? Almost as dark as you. It's hard to imagine she's half Chinese.'

Aunt Mona said this with a smile, but in a voice that sounded as though she expected them to be angry with her, but neither

Lizhi nor her mother minded.

People had said Lizhi looked funny before. Usually they said it to each other, as though they thought Lizhi did not understand English or French or Mandarin or whatever language they were speaking. Lizhi's father had explained it to her. 'Nothing at all wrong with how you look. You are the most beautiful girl in the whole world—except for your mum of course—and everyone else is jealous!'

Her father would always talk like that. Her mother called it 'Michael's nonsense' but she smiled when she said it and Lizhi could tell she liked it even if she called it nonsense.

And even if he had been joking, whenever anyone said anything about how Lizhi looked she remembered her father grinning as he called her beautiful and that made her feel good inside.

Still her mother hesitated, 'I was hoping Lizhi could meet her grandfather. It was Michael's last wish, you know ... perhaps if you tell me which hospital he's in I could just take Lizhi there to meet him. We wouldn't have to stay for long—and then I'll find some way to cancel my China trip and—'

Aunt Mona cut through her words.

'I really don't know what you're hoping to get out of this, Juliette!'

'Take these bags to the back room,' Aunt Mona ordered Bwe

Bwe without looking at her and without any change in tone.

'I'll do that—' Lizhi's Mother said. 'If you just tell me where—'

'Don't be ridiculous!' Aunt Mona snapped. 'It's what she's paid to do. Now with the old man away she has nothing to do with herself all day. She knows that I'm not keeping her here if there's nothing for her to do so she better pull her weight!'

Lizhi thought Bwe Bwe could not have much weight to pull. Bwe Bwe was skinny and not much taller than Lizhi but she was strong. Quite easily she picked up one of the bags and slung it over her shoulder. Then she took the handle of her father's suitcase (which had rollers on the bottom) and pulled it after her. Lizhi picked up her own backpack and started to follow her. Lizhi thought that if Bwe Bwe had nothing to do with herself she might be willing to show her around the house, and perhaps tomorrow they could play together.

'Your daughter seems to think it is more important to play servant than to say hello to me,' Aunt Mona observed.

'That was very unfair,' Lizhi thought. 'I already said hello to you,' she pointed out to Aunt Mona. She turned but kept walking backwards after Bwe Bwe. 'And I'm not playing servant. I'm just taking care of my own things. Mama said I should always take care of my own things.'

Aunt Mona did not answer her. Instead she said to Juliette. 'If I'm going to be responsible for the girl while you are in China I must take responsibility for teaching her some manners. You've clearly allowed her to run wild. What time does your flight leave?'

At the top of the stairs Bwe Bwe insisted on taking all the bags herself. 'Mam say I take.' Lizhi decided she could get to know her later. Besides it had just occurred to her she ought to spend as much time as possible with her mother before she left.

'You can't just wash your hands of her, you know,' Lizhi heard Aunt Mona say. 'My father would never agree to that. He said that just because that brother of mine was irresponsible enough to bring unnecessary children into the world when he could barely support himself doesn't mean we have to support them—'

'I don't want to leave her here!' Juliette said quickly. She sounded alarmed. 'Just for five days—and because I promised Michael I would bring Lizhi to meet his family. And I can support her very well; I'm not asking for money.'

Aunt Mona did not say anything but the way she raised her eyebrows and twisted the corners of her mouth made Lizhi think that she did not believe what her mother had said.

'Excuse me, but I understood the reason why you asked if the girl could stay here was because you don't have a home to leave her in—or anyone else to leave her with. I also understood you could not afford to miss this trip to China because you need the money they're offering you. I don't suppose you have somehow managed to acquire a home for this child since that conversation on the telephone, so am I to assume you've come into money since then—unless you had some reason for lying to me?'

'No—no. Not at all. I just—no. What I said then—that's all true.'

Lizhi hated to see her mother look so guilty and unhappy.

'Papa and Mama had lots of money,' she said firmly. 'But Papa's hospital treatment cost a lot. They were trying to save his life and he had three operations in three days. And then Mama said it was no use saving Papa's body when his spirit had already gone. But hospitals cost a lot of money. That's why she has to go to China to see the people who want to pay a lot of money for Papa's paintings.' Ordinarily this would have been 'talking back' to adults and Aunt Mona would have disapproved; but the mention of China and money seemed to remind the adults why they were there.

'Well you mustn't miss your flight,' Aunt Mona said. 'I hope you know what you're doing. Don't just give everything away because you need quick money now. You have to think of the future, you know. Have you had his work—whatever you're selling—professionally evaluated?'

Lizhi had never heard anyone speak to her mother like that. People usually came to her to ask her to tell them what their artwork was worth. After all, before Lizhi was born, she had worked in universities teaching people about art. To her surprise, her mother only nodded now, and said, 'Yes, you're right, of course. You are right. I don't understand the business side of things. But I have a friend coming with me—Michael's friend really. Jeremiah is a lawyer and a businessman and he'll make sure we get a good deal.'

'You artists are so idealistic!' Aunt Mona said. 'You can't just trust anybody. Just because this Jeremiah was Michael's friend doesn't mean he won't try to swindle you. And while we're on the subject, you can't go running around the world with strange men,' Aunt Mona said. 'It's unstable and unsafe. If you want to be a decent mother to this girl you have to do some serious thinking and start making some serious changes to your lifestyle!'

There was a pause after this. It was clear they were all thinking of her father because when Aunt Mona spoke again, she said, 'I hope he didn't suffer too much.'

'Well, he was unconscious,' Juliette said. 'He never woke up after the accident. I suppose I was hoping for the best right till the end, no matter what the doctors said ... I told him to rest and to sleep until he was ready to wake up—but he never woke up. He promised me he was going to take a rest stop after the

Austrian project was completed …' she broke off. Lizhi's father had completed the Austrian wall paintings only two days before he was hit by the car.

Lizhi saw an old man standing near the gate. He was holding a stick and watching them. Lizhi thought he must be the old gardener her father had mentioned. She wondered whether he remembered her father. If she got the chance she would tell the old man that her father had remembered him. She waved at him but he turned away and disappeared into the trees.

When the taxi came back to take Juliette to the airport Lizhi saw the old gardener again. He stood at a distance and watched.

'I'll be back for you in less than a week, my precious,' her mother promised her. 'Five days will pass in no time. You won't miss me at all. I'll be back before you know I'm gone.'

But that was not true. Even as she saw the back lights of the taxi blink on red as it paused at the gate before turning out to the main road, she already missed her mother so much it was like a twisting pain in her stomach. But Lizhi reminded herself that she was brave. With all the other things her mother had to worry about she did not want her to have to worry about her daughter as well.

'Where's my room?' Lizhi asked Aunt Mona.

LIZHI'S FATHER'S HOUSE

The house Lizhi's father grew up in was a huge mess. Once Lizhi went in she guessed that was the reason why Aunt Mona had not invited her mother inside. Even in the big front room there was no place for a visitor to sit down. It was a big room—the whole house was huge—but it looked as though there were several sets of furniture and at least two dining tables all pushed in together, with several cupboards and screens as well. There was no place to sit except for two chairs at one corner of one of the dining tables. The rest of the table was piled high with books and folders and boxes. It was hard to see what colour the walls were because there were so many shelves and cupboards. The floor was made of planks of wood that squeaked when you stepped on them.

'What are you staring at?' Aunt Mona had asked sharply when Lizhi stood and stared.

'It's a nice room,' Lizhi said politely. Her mother had taught her that when going to other people's houses for the first time you should always say something nice about the place. 'It's got very good light and it's airy.' Lizhi was not sure what this meant but when her father or mother said it people usually seemed pleased.

It worked. Aunt Mona stopped looking defensive and almost smiled. 'It does,' she said. 'It's the high ceilings. They don't build houses like this anymore. They don't build houses for you anymore unless you are some kind of millionaire or billionaire; they want us all to go and live in those ridiculous little boxes stuck up in the sky …' She stopped herself. 'Anyway, you should go and wash up … Do you need to use the um—'

'Oh I went at the airport,' Lizhi said. 'Papa always said to pee whenever you can; no point carrying extra weight around.'

'There's no need to keep bringing your father into

everything,' Aunt Mona said. 'Anyway, go and tell Bwe Bwe to unpack for you.'

The house was not dirty—there was no dust and no bugs that Lizhi could see but while it did not smell bad there was a heavy scent of old things. It looked as though years and years of things were crowded into every room.

Even the room that Lizhi was supposed to sleep in was crowded with furniture. It was a small room with a small, very high bed with a clean white sheet tucked tightly in. There were also cupboards all around the walls and boxes full of papers and shoes and cloth scraps and clothes hangers.

The doors to most of the other rooms were locked.

'No need to clean,' Bwe Bwe explained to her. Even Bwe Bwe's shyness or fear could not stand up to Lizhi's friendliness—at least when Aunt Mona was not around. When Aunt Mona was around Bwe Bwe did not talk to Lizhi at all. 'Inside is all things from long ago. Keep safe inside so no need to go in to clean.'

Lizhi soon came to realise Aunt Mona never threw anything away. Even the receipt from the taxi that Juliette had dropped was picked up by Aunt Mona and carefully folded and put away in a box.

'Why?' Lizhi asked Aunt Mona when they sat down to lunch at the small space at the corner of the dining table.

'Why what?'

'Why are you keeping that?'

'You never know. I might need a record of when your mother brought you here. Or she might want to check how much the driver charged her. You can't trust taxi drivers here.'

Aunt Mona didn't seem to trust anybody.

She always seemed to be scolding Bwe Bwe for doing things too slowly or doing things wrong or not doing things she should have done even if she hadn't been told.

Lizhi thought that if nothing was ever thrown away in this house there was a good chance that some of the things might already have been there when her father was a boy. But it was no use asking Aunt Mona about that.

'Don't bother me with things like that,' was all Aunt Mona would say.

Lizhi saw the gardener sometimes too, but the old man always watched from a distance. Bwe Bwe told her that the old man lived in a small house at the far corner of the property. When Lizhi asked Bwe Bwe if she knew him and what his name was Bwe Bwe just giggled nervously. Sometimes Lizhi found it difficult to tell whether Bwe Bwe could not understand her English or did not know the answers to her questions.

It was not surprising that Bwe Bwe was scared of talking. Aunt Mona was even fiercer to her than she was to Lizhi. She tried to speak nicely to Lizhi but she got pretty impatient sometimes. Then, because she did not want to scold Lizhi, she would find some reason to scold Bwe Bwe.

Bwe Bwe was scared of Aunt Mona and Lizhi knew that sometimes after she got a scolding she would go to her room at the back of the kitchen to cry.

Sometimes Aunt Mona tried to be nice to Lizhi.

'Do you know your parents named you after a fruit?' Aunt Mona said to Lizhi on the second morning she was there. 'We must get some lychees for you to try. Do you know what a lychee is? You should try some. Then when your mother comes back for you, you can tell her that you know where your name comes from!'

Aunt Mona tightened her mouth sideways to show Lizhi that she was making a joke.

'I'm not named after a fruit,' Lizhi said. 'My parents gave me a Chinese name because I'm half Chinese. "Lizhi" comes from "Li" meaning beautiful and "Zhi" meaning wisdom.'

Aunt Mona stared at Lizhi, her mouth open. Then she closed her mouth and looked cross. 'How did those parents of yours come up with something like that? I know my brother. Michael was never any good at Chinese. He was worse than me!' She seemed angry, as though she had uncovered an impostor. 'Did they pay some kind of fortune-teller or feng shui person to come up with a name for you?'

'They were both studying Mandarin with me,' Lizhi explained. 'Like they were both studying French. They wanted me to be in touch with my roots so this way we could all speak Mandarin and French—'

'Ridiculous!' muttered Aunt Mona.

Lizhi looked at Aunt Mona curiously. 'Mama said you are a school teacher. What do you teach?' she asked. 'What is it like in school in Singapore? Can I come to classes while I'm staying here?' Lizhi only wanted to know because she was always curious about what schools were like. Lizhi knew her mother worried sometimes about Lizhi not going to school. Even though Lizhi was learning many other things from travelling, whenever her father had been based in one place for at least a month her mother had arranged for her to sit in for classes. Lizhi thought that perhaps Aunt Mona could arrange for Lizhi to do that in Singapore since she was a schoolteacher.

For some reason this question seemed to make Aunt Mona even more cross than usual.

'The girl doesn't know anything at all!' Aunt Mona said to the ceiling since there was no one else in the room. 'Go and play or do something useful,' she said to Lizhi. 'Don't bother me. I'm busy.'

It was difficult to find anything to do in the house. Bwe Bwe was always working and Aunt Mona did not like it when Lizhi tried to help her. Lizhi tried to occupy herself but there was not much to do, no books for children and no one to play with. She only saw Aunt Mona at mealtimes though she had a habit of appearing suddenly if Lizhi tried to get Bwe Bwe to play with her, which made Bwe Bwe even more nervous and reluctant.

'Did the old gardener know my father?' Lizhi asked Aunt Mona at breakfast on the third day she was there.

'Old gardener?'

Lizhi nodded. 'I saw him. The old man outside.'

Aunt Mona made a strange, straining sound. It sounded to Lizhi as if Aunt Mona needed to go to the toilet in a hurry.

'You stay away from him, you hear? He's not safe to be around. He gambles and drinks and he is a bad influence. And more than a bit psycho. I want you to stay away from him, you hear?'

Lizhi nodded but she kept her fingers crossed behind her. She wondered where the old gardener went to gamble and drink.

But most of the time at mealtimes it was Aunt Mona who asked the questions.

'Your mother and father—so you don't know if they own a house anywhere?'

Or

'Who is the man that your mother is going to China with?

This Jeremiah fellow. How well does your mother know him? Is he also black?'

Lizhi didn't have answers to most of these questions and Aunt Mona did not like the answers that Lizhi did give her.

'He's more the same colour as me,' Lizhi said. 'But I think he's Chinese like Papa.'

BETWEEN MEALS

Five days was less than one week and should not have felt like a very long time. But five days of three meals a day was fifteen meals and for Lizhi that was the hardest part of staying in Singapore. Her father had talked a lot about how wonderful Singapore food was, but Lizhi did not think so at all.

All that Aunt Mona and Bwe Bwe seemed to eat was instant noodles. Lizhi ate instant noodles for every meal for her first two days and then she said, 'Can't I have something else?'

Aunt Mona stressed, 'I told you I can't stand picky eaters. We are not rich, you know! Anyway, you can choose which flavour you want. There's Chicken Curry and there's Pepper Crab.'

But there was no chicken curry or pepper crab in the noodles. Those were just the labels on the seasoning packets that Bwe Bwe shook over and stirred into the cooked noodles.

'I can eat bread,' Lizhi suggested.

Plain bread was not something Lizhi normally liked to eat but after all the instant noodles for lunch and dinner she felt it would be very good to eat bread.

But Aunt Mona said bread was only for breakfast.

It was not so bad for Aunt Mona because she went out for meals sometimes and Lizhi was sure that she didn't eat instant noodles then.

One day when two women came to take Aunt Mona out to lunch with them she called Lizhi out to the porch to say 'hello' though she did not tell her who she was supposed to say hello to. It was clear they had been talking about her.

'Look at that hair!' One of them said. All three women giggled.

'She doesn't look anything like Michael, does she?' They giggled again. 'Can't see anything of Michael in her!'

'Did you know my father?' Lizhi asked, quite reasonably,

she thought. Then added, 'Where are you going for lunch? Can I come with you?' She knew it was not polite to ask for things but she was tired of having no one to talk to, 'I would like to see more of Singapore.'

For some reason Aunt Mona and her friends seemed to find this very funny as well.

'That accent!' One of the women said.

'Mother's supposed to be French,' Aunt Mona rolled her eyes. 'Anyway I showed you the stuff Michael sent back ...'

They didn't take Lizhi to lunch with them. She had a feeling that they wanted to talk about her and her mother but as her mother would have said, it was no use imagining things. Lizhi knew how to telephone for pizza but the only phone in the house was Aunt Mona's mobile that she kept with her all the time and had taken with her. 'Who do you want to call?' Aunt Mona asked suspiciously when Lizhi asked if she could borrow it. 'If your mother wants to talk to you she can call me. Don't waste money on long-distance calls.'

It was easier to talk to Bwe Bwe when Aunt Mona was not there.

'I am fifteen years old,' Bwe Bwe told Lizhi when Aunt Mona was out. 'But to come to Singapore to work a person has to be eighteen years old, so in Singapore I am eighteen years old.'

Also, when Aunt Mona was out, Lizhi and Bwe Bwe could

eat the mangoes and bananas that the old man (who Bwe Bwe agreed did some gardening) left on the bench behind the kitchen door. Lizhi was very curious about this old man. She had not seen him after the first day. He didn't live in the house but in a wooden shed built next to what Bwe Bwe said used to be an outhouse. An outhouse was what people used before modern toilets were built. When Aunt Mona was out, Bwe Bwe showed the little two-room shelter to Lizhi—it was a few hundred yards from the house, against the seawall that separated the back garden from the shore and the mangrove swamp. That was where the old man stayed, Bwe Bwe said. He did his own cleaning and cooking and she had never been inside the little house. There were two windows on each side but there was cloth pinned over them and even standing on tiptoe and pushing aside the cloth Lizhi could not see much inside. It was very small and much less cluttered than the rest of the house. There was a bed, a desk, a bookshelf and some gardening tools.

'Why doesn't he stay in the big house?' Lizhi asked. There were so many rooms in the house.

'He won't go inside the big house anymore,' Bwe Bwe said. 'Ever since—' then she stopped and looked scared. 'We better go back now. Or else Madam will come back and be angry.' Bwe Bwe was scared of Aunt Mona even when she was not there. When she looked scared like that Lizhi knew there was nothing she could do except return to the house.

When Aunt Mona got back that afternoon she was all excited, like Lizhi's father used to be when he was about to make a breakthrough in a painting. Even as she was taking off her shoes her phone rang and she wedged her mobile phone to her ear with her shoulder and said, 'Look I just got home, I haven't found anything yet. And anyway I told you, I don't know what Ah Ma went and told Michael. She was talking nonsense about wanting to put things right but I am sure she didn't manage to see or talk to anybody. She didn't use my phone and I know she can't have sent anything by mail. It would have had to go through me. She hadn't left the house on her own for years!'

Aunt Mona had a habit of walking around the house talking on her phone. It was good because when she was talking it was easy to tell where she was, and she did not bother so much about what Bwe Bwe and Lizhi were doing. Sometimes Lizhi tried to listen, just in case Aunt Mona happened to be talking to her mother. Then if her mother asked to talk to Lizhi she would be right there and ready. But this time because she had heard her father's name she wanted to listen all the more.

'No. That so-called wife of Michael didn't say anything about the will. Anyway, there's no way she can know anything. I have the only copy of Ma's will safe here with me. It was made long before Michael met that woman so it doesn't matter what Ma may have told Michael or what Michael told her. If they don't have something down on paper it's not going to count!' Aunt Mona said.

She turned and started walking back up the corridor towards Lizhi. Lizhi stayed very still. Luckily there was a cupboard placed on top of a table behind stacks of newspapers so Lizhi sat quietly behind the newspapers and Aunt Mona walked past without noticing her. 'Some people just grab, grab, grab with no shame! But they're not going to get anything out of us!'

Lizhi didn't think it was fair of Aunt Mona to talk about her or her mother that way because neither of them had tried to grab anything from Aunt Mona. Even though the house was stuffed full of things Lizhi had not yet seen anything she wanted to grab and grab.

Still talking into her phone, Aunt Mona went halfway up the stairs to the second floor. She took out a key and unlocked the door on the landing, behind a stack of magazines and shoeboxes. Lizhi crept up the stairs and looked in. Like all the other rooms in the house this one was full of shelves and cupboards and boxes. Aunt Mona, with her back to Lizhi, was still on the phone. Lizhi watched as she took a box file from one of the cupboards and slammed it on top of the pile already on the bed. The dust made her cough. But without wasting any time she grabbed a couple of brown envelopes from the box and started to read from some papers inside them to the person on the phone.

Lizhi recognised what Aunt Mona was reading as what her father had called 'lawyer talk'. It was the kind of talk that people used when they had to deal with large amounts of money—the kind of talk her mother needed Uncle Jeremiah to help her deal with in China.

'I want to have everything clear and sorted out by the time she gets back,' Aunt Mona said into the phone. 'That's in three more days' time. Not that I have to, but I want to have an answer to give her if she brings it up. I don't know what kind of ideas Ma went and put into Michael's head!'

Aunt Mona shuffled more envelopes, sounding more and more cross. Then she turned back to the door and Lizhi moved out of the way just in time. It was lucky there was so much furniture all over the house because Aunt Mona would have seen her if there hadn't been a chest of drawers and bundles of old curtains and towels for Lizhi to move behind.

Aunt Mona did not lock the door behind her. In fact she stumbled over some shoes and slippers on the landing and left the door standing open. Lizhi reasoned that since she had not been told to not go in she could. From the doorway she had seen some drawings and some little wood carvings that looked interesting.

Once inside the room Lizhi ignored the box on the bed and went straight to the drawings taped on the wall. They were in pencil and charcoal and some looked like they had been done with pastel sticks like her father had used for drawing. Lizhi wondered whether he had drawn them years ago when he lived in this house. But even more interesting were the pieces of wood and coral that were in open baskets and plastic bags. Some looked like natural pieces of driftwood but others were carved into little boats and miniature trees. Maybe some of these were her father's. They were the kind of things he had always liked. Most of the drawers in the room were locked, but the cupboard from which Aunt Mona had taken the box file stood partly open and there were more photographs and drawings in there. Lizhi liked drawings but she preferred them taped to walls or the fridge rather than hidden in envelopes. Then she found a small green cloth bag. Inside there was a tiny mudskipper. It seemed to have been carved out of a piece of dark stone but the deep red shining eyes looked like they were made with glass. Though small it was heavy and fitted comfortably into Lizhi's palm. Her fingers curled around it as though it belonged there. The different colours in the translucent stone made the tiny sculpture look like it had browns and blacks in its skin.

Though Lizhi had never seen a real mudskipper before she knew what the tiny statue was at once because her father used to paint mudskippers. In fact, her father used to call her his little mudskipper.

Lizhi wondered if the mudskipper belonged to Aunt Mona. She did not look like the kind of person who liked animal toys but then it was hard to tell. One of Lizhi's parents' friends was a university professor who taught very difficult subjects but collected tiny models of animals and miniature tea sets. These things looked like toys to Lizhi (she would have loved to play with them) but because they belonged to adults they were considered 'collector's items' or 'art' and were not to be played with.

Lizhi thought that was probably how Aunt Mona saw the sweet brown mudskipper. If only she had been a friendlier sort of aunt Lizhi would have asked if she could play with the little mudskipper for a while, and Aunt Mona might even have said something like, 'Why don't I give it to you? After all I haven't given you any birthday presents ever so even though this mudskipper is a valuable collector's item and work of art I will give it to you as all your birthday—and Christmas—presents added up.'

But though Lizhi found it very easy to imagine how an aunt might want to give her the sweet little statue she could not imagine Aunt Mona doing it.

The little mudskipper had felt cold to the touch when she picked it up, but now the heat of her little hand made it warm and much harder to put down.

She could just borrow it for a while, Lizhi decided. It was not stealing if she put it back before anyone noticed. Lizhi just wanted to take the little mudskipper outdoors and play with it on the grass, outdoors where there was light. After all, it must be tired of being stuck in a cloth bag in the dark.

'I'll bring you back,' she whispered to the mudskipper before she tucked it back into its little cloth bag.

Lizhi was so engrossed she almost did not hear Aunt Mona coming back. Luckily for her Aunt Mona was still preoccupied with her phone call.

'No,' Aunt Mona was saying, 'the child doesn't know anything—' Lizhi crouched down behind two mattresses propped up against the wall. Aunt Mona did not see her, but that might not have been a good thing because Aunt Mona slammed some envelopes back into the box, then walked out of the room—and closed and locked the door behind her.

It could have been worse, Lizhi reflected, after Aunt Mona's footsteps and voice faded into the distance. She wondered how long it would be till Aunt Mona came to look for something else in the room, or till Bwe Bwe came to clean it … but then Bwe Bwe had said she didn't have to clean the locked rooms.

THE GARDENER AND THE GARDEN

Fortunately there was a window. And when Lizhi, standing on the bed, managed to push it open she saw there was a ledge running around the house just below the window and there was a thick mass of tangled shrubbery and bushes and weeds just below that.

Lizhi climbed out of the window, steadied herself on the ledge with one arm over the windowsill and half jumped, half fell into the shrubbery. She landed with more of a rustling bounce than a bang and knew that apart from a few scratches she was safe. It was such a relief that Lizhi lay there for a moment laughing out loud. She had forgotten how much fun it was to climb and jump and explore.

Then she felt someone watching her. Lizhi sat up and saw the old man she had seen before. Close up Lizhi saw his skin was tanned dark brown from the sun but he looked Chinese.

'What do you think you are doing?'

Lizhi scrambled to get out of the bushes and back onto her feet. She thought it should have been obvious that she was getting out of the house through the window.

Lizhi had already decided the man must be the gardener her father had told her about. She had looked around for him before but never found him. Now he was standing there with his stick, looking down at her.

Lizhi scrambled to her feet. 'Are you the gardener?' she asked him eagerly. 'I've seen your house. But you weren't there when I went to look. My father told me about you. He grew up here. His name was Michael Wang. He said you were already working here when he was growing up. Do you remember my father?'

'And who are you?' the old man asked without answering Lizhi's question.

'I'm Lizhi Wang.' Lizhi remembered her manners. 'Pleased to meet you. What's your name?'

'Why do you want to know?' the old man asked.

'I can't go on calling you Mr Gardener,' Lizhi said. 'Or I could, I suppose, if you prefer it.' The old man was the first gardener Lizhi had met so she was not sure how gardeners felt about such things.

'Luckily you landed in the bougainvillea,' the old man said. 'You could have broken an arm or a leg otherwise.'

'So what's your name?' Lizhi asked.

The old man looked confused and did not answer for a moment. 'Stubborn, aren't you?' he said finally.

Lizhi laughed, 'How can you not know your own name?' she asked. 'Anyway, I just need something to call you by.'

'You can call me Grandpa,' the old man suggested. 'I'm about the right age.'

'No, I can't. I hate my grandfather,' Lizhi said firmly. 'Why do you live in that wooden house?'

'You are full of questions, aren't you?' the old man said. But he said it as though he had just learned something new about her rather than as a scolding.

'I don't know much about Singapore,' Lizhi admitted. 'Even

though I'm half Singaporean. That's why I have to ask questions. But Bwe Bwe doesn't speak much English and Aunt Mona doesn't have time.'

'What do you want to know?'

Lizhi gave a small sigh of pleasure. With everything that was going on in her life it was a long time since an adult had had the time to answer all the questions Lizhi had and the number of things she wanted to know was growing. But now she was not sure where to start until she remembered—

'What does Neo Tiew mean?' Lizhi asked. 'You know, like the road outside.'

He looked curiously at her.

'Why do you want to know?'

This was a question that Lizhi always found difficult to answer—not because she didn't know the answer but because the answer seemed so obvious to her that she could not understand why anyone would ask.

'Because I don't know what it means,' she said.

Unlike so many other grown-ups, the old man nodded as though this made sense to him.

'I also wondered once,' he said. 'I had to ask people to find out. That was before there was internet to look up everything. Long ago a man named Neo Tiew founded the Lim Chu Kang village. He was the sheriff of the village, which was on the banks of the Sungei Kranji—that means the Kranji River.'

'So "sungei" means "river"?'

'Yes,' the old man did not seem to mind being interrupted. In fact he seemed pleased that Lizhi was interested enough to comment. 'Neo Tiew also set up a primary school and health centre in the village. That's why the roads are named after him.'

'Is the primary school still there?' Lizhi asked. 'I have to go to school soon,' she explained.

'Oh, that was years and years ago,' the old man said. 'In those days all this—' he waved his arm to indicate the space around them, '—this whole place was pepper and gambier and rubber plantations. But they are all gone now. The school is gone too. Things are always changing in Singapore.'

'I know,' Lizhi said. 'Papa said that in the old days the sea came right up to the wall behind the house and when it was high tide he could climb into his boat through the gate in the back wall. I wish I had a boat. Did you know my Papa?'

'Did your Papa tell you why he did that?'

Lizhi thought that having a boat of your own was reason enough for anyone to want to climb into it. But then she remembered something else. 'He used to go over to the mangrove swamps when it was high tide,' she said. 'When it was low tide he would walk over, otherwise he went in the boat. When it was high tide the big fishes would come in with the current, and during low tide he would see the small fishes and the crabs and the mudskippers.'

'I like mudskippers,' she added, remembering the little stone figure hidden in the room. Lizhi had left it behind. When climbing out of windows it is not a good idea to have too many things on you.

'What else did your father tell you about Singapore?'

Lizhi thought about this. Over the years her father had told her so many things about Singapore that it was difficult to pick on any one thing.

'My father told me that Singapore food is great, because it has got everything in the world but it's not true. All that Singapore people eat for every meal is instant noodles. And I hate them.'

'Do you want to try some other Singapore food?'

'Oh yes please! But Bwe Bwe says there's nowhere nearby to eat and Aunt Mona has the only phone so we can't even call for pizza.'

'I'll take you to a place where you can try some Singapore food. There is a shortcut but we have to go through the mangroves. Do you think you can do that?'

'Oh yes please!' Lizhi's eyes were shining. She was even more excited by the thought of exploring the mangrove swamps than of finally having something different to eat.

'And you can call me Ah Guan,' the old man said.

OUTSIDE

Aunt Mona had never told Lizhi that she could not leave the house and garden—but then that was probably because it had never occurred to her that she might do that. Lizhi was sure that even as a child her Aunt Mona must have been the sort of girl who never got her dresses or shoes dirty and always had clean fingernails. That was probably why Aunt Mona found it so difficult to understand Lizhi, who was not that sort of girl at all.

Most of the garden, beyond the back porch and cement path of the house, was an exciting tangle of bushes and creepers. Lizhi and Ah Guan walked across the garden to the end of it. There was a low stone wall and beyond that were rocks sloping downwards.

'We are going by the shortcut over the mangrove swamps and rocks,' Ah Guan said. 'Here it is important to keep an eye on the tides. No matter how good you are at climbing or swimming, people can only cross at this point at low tide.'

'What happens at high tide?' Lizhi asked.

'At high tide people have to go the long way around by road. But that will take a long time because the army does training around here and they don't allow people to just cut across. So are you game?'

'Oh yes!' said Lizhi. She had not had this much fun since coming to Singapore. But then Lizhi remembered her dress.

Her mother had packed all her nice dresses for Singapore because she wanted Lizhi to make a good impression on her grandfather and aunt. Her mother could not have guessed that her grandfather would not want to see her and Aunt Mona would never take her out, which meant Lizhi had to wear her party dresses in the house. Lizhi did not mind that but she did not think a white dress with a pattern of pink carnations on it and a pink ribbon made to look like a string of carnations tied around her waist was a good dress to explore mangrove swamps in. Even she could see that. Her mother had told her so many times that pretty frocks were not to be worn while playing in mud, in water, up trees or even for riding down slides or climbing up ropes.

It seemed to Lizhi that there was really no good reason for wearing pretty frocks—unless it was to impress people. But Aunt Mona had not been impressed and her grandfather didn't want to see her so the pretty frock was no good to her at all.

'I have to take off my dress first,' Lizhi told Ah Guan.

He did not seem surprised. Unlike most of the other grown-ups Lizhi had met so far he had not said 'Why?' and 'No!' almost before she finished saying what she wanted to.

'What will you wear?' he asked.

'I have my undies,' Lizhi explained. 'A vest, and I'm wearing shorts over my knickers just in case. Quite good enough for the swamp. Then if I get them muddy I can put the dress back on and it won't show. And anyway it's too stiff.' The dress was stiff because Lizhi's mother had starched it and ironed it very carefully. But even if that made it good to look at it didn't make it very comfortable to wear. Lizhi took her dress off carefully and Ah Guan hung it on the branch of a tree for her.

Very carefully Lizhi followed Ah Guan down the path across the rocks and then down to the water's edge. The old man walked slowly, pausing to check that Lizhi was following him without any trouble. Lizhi, slipping and splashing occasionally, managed to keep up very well. She had to get used to walking on the different textures of damp sand and dead leaves, but he saw she was confident, learned quickly and was not afraid of getting wet. He would probably have turned back if Lizhi had shown any sign of distress, but as it was they continued comfortably.

Her father had liked talking about the mangrove swamps but Lizhi had not really listened because it was the sort of thing he told her about when he put her to bed at night and she was falling asleep. He would tell Lizhi about how the roots of the trees grew out of the mud and how you could see fish and snakes and snails in the water ...

'I know that the mangrove swamps are where seawater and freshwater meet,' Lizhi said, pleased to remember this fact. 'At high tide, when the water comes in from the sea then it's salt water, and at low tide when the water comes out of the canals and rivers then it's freshwater. And the animals and plants there can survive in both saltwater and freshwater.'

'That's very good,' the old man said. 'You are absolutely right. Would you like to see some of the mangrove animals and plants yourself?'

Of course Lizhi would. More than anything.

'Your father used to love the mangrove swamp too,' Ah Guan said.

'So you did know him,' Lizhi said. 'I used to ask him about them because they were his favourite thing to paint,' Lizhi explained. 'But he's dead now.'

'Long long ago,' Ah Guan said. 'He used to spend all his free time out here.' He was talking more to himself than to Lizhi. 'I never thought he could ever tear himself away from this place. Then once he left he never came back.' His voice trailed off. Then suddenly he froze and very softly said, 'Look. Over at the base of that tree. There, you see? That's a mudskipper.'

Lizhi saw something move. It was small and brown and not shiny at all. She was not very impressed.

'Is that all? Why isn't it bigger?'

'How much bigger do you want it to be?' the man asked.

Lizhi thought. She held her hands out as wide as she could. 'This big,' she said. 'Then I could ride on it. And I could go into the water on its back.'

Ah Guan laughed. 'Then it wouldn't be a mudskipper. It would be a freak. People at the Resorts World would put it in a tank and charge us money to look at it and the traditional Chinese medicine people would cut it up and sell it to make cancer cures and love potions.'

'That's horrible,' Lizhi said. 'To be a freak like that and not belong to one place or another.'

Ah Guan seemed surprised to hear her say this. 'Why? It

could mean you are at home in both the places.'

'But it doesn't happen like that in real life,' Lizhi said.

Ah Guan seemed to want to know more, and Lizhi was always happy to talk.

'It's like me,' she said. 'Papa used to call me his little mudskipper and he and Mama like me as I am. But everyone here thinks I'm weird. Like Aunt Mona and her friends.'

The old man looked surprised. 'Why did your father call you a mudskipper?'

Anyone else would probably have been too embarrassed to say, but Lizhi liked answering questions almost as much as she liked asking them.

'Because I get muddy no matter where I go,' she said honestly. Looking down at her hands and feet and her little undershirt and shorts they both could see how true this was. 'But also because of me being half and half, you see. Like a mudskipper. I don't belong in the water and I don't belong on the land.'

The old man nodded. Lizhi crouched down to get a closer look at the mudskipper. She was having a great time and was getting very muddy. The old man didn't seem to mind. He crouched down and got muddy too. Lizhi wanted so much to take a mudskipper back to show her mother but the old man said it was not a good idea to take creatures out of their natural habitat.

'I could keep it alive in a tank,' Lizhi said.

'I don't think it works like that,' the old man said. 'Would you like to be kept in a tank? That's not how we do things here.' He stood up and started walking again. Startled, the little mudskipper vanished into the mud.

Lizhi remembered the little stone mudskipper in its green cloth bag. It was certainly not in its habitat there so what Ah Guan said was not true.

'Anyway, here we are—'

They had arrived at the crossing point. Ah Guan pointed to where a large rock on the shore extended out into the water almost like a giant tooth. There was a handwritten sign on a stick, covered in plastic that said 'Caution. Danger.' It did not look very dangerous to Lizhi who was used to climbing over smooth rocks. Some of the rocks here were slippery with moss even though the tide was low. Lizhi had to hold onto the sign to climb around it, with Ah Guan steadying her from behind.

Once beyond the sign they could no longer see the house or any other sign of life except for an old makeshift shrine halfway up the rocks. The beach was deserted, and when Lizhi stopped walking she heard soft whirring clicks coming out of the many tiny holes in the damp sand. Ah Guan gestured to her to stay still. After what felt like a long long time staring at the holes in the damp sand Lizhi saw the hermit crabs emerge. They started crawling around on the sand.

Ah Guan picked up one of the hermit crabs. 'Look. This one has outgrown its shell,' he said. 'Soon it will have to find a new one to move into.' Startled, the creature tried to withdraw into its shell but it was already so large that parts of its legs stuck out.

'Hermit crabs don't grow their own shells. They look for vacant shells left behind by sea snails and move in. It's like recycling. And they aren't real crabs.'

'Then it's stupid to call them crabs,' Lizhi said.

'What do you want to call them?'

'Well, what are they?' Lizhi asked.

'Decapod crustaceans,' the old man said. 'Decapod because "deca" means ten and pod refers to their feet. They are ten-footed crustaceans.'

Lizhi thought about this. 'Maybe it's easier to call them hermit crabs,' she agreed. Sometimes, as long as people knew what they were talking about, it was not necessary to be too precise. The hermit crab, realising it had not been eaten, had come out of its shell and was exploring Ah Guan's palm.

'They operate vacancy chains.' Ah Guan put the hermit crab back on the sand. 'When a new, bigger shell becomes available, hermit crabs gather around it and form a kind of queue from largest to smallest. When the largest crab moves into the new shell, the second biggest crab moves into the newly vacated shell, thereby making its previous shell available to the third crab, and so on.'

It was a lovely image. Lizhi could just imagine all the crabs lining up and moving into their new homes.

'People should move out of houses in that way too,' Lizhi said, thinking of the great big house that only Aunt Mona and Bwe Bwe were now living in. 'Move out of houses that are too big or too small. If Aunt Mona moved into a smaller house then Bwe Bwe wouldn't have to work so hard.'

Ah Guan nodded to acknowledge this. Then he asked, 'Where will you and your mother be going next?'

Lizhi started to answer, then realised she didn't know. In the old days her father had always talked to her mother and her about his painting projects and where they would go next. When he had some time between jobs they all got very excited because he loved going to new places for exhibitions and meeting other artists. 'Iceland or Japan?' Lizhi remembered him asking her mother. 'The Reykjavik Arts Festival has the Iceland Symphonic Orchestra playing and there will be outdoor painting with live models, but we've never been to Japan before—this Kitakyushu Festival looks interesting too …'

Lizhi's mother would laugh at how excited he got. He was like a little boy, she said. But Lizhi's father had died before they could go to either Iceland or Japan. He would never get to see

Japan now.

Lizhi felt sad again.

'Come,' Ah Guan said, thinking she was tired. 'I promised you something Singapore style to eat, right? We just have to go up through that path there and across that section of the swamp, and we will be at the road that leads to the jetty. That is where the fishermen and ferry people eat before going to and from the offshore islands by boat.'

SINGAPORE FOOD

Coming through the path from the swamp they came to a road that led to a giant concrete square and beyond that to a pier that extended into the sea. There was a row of low wooden buildings on each side of the square, with awnings extended to shelter the walkway from the sun. Beyond this boats bobbed gently on the water or were pulled up on the sand. They were small wooden boats, some of them with nets and clothes drying on top of them.

'Why aren't there any people in the boats?' Lizhi asked.

'It's the wrong time of day,' Ah Guan said. 'The fishermen go out early in the morning or late at night to fish. And people who come to Singapore to work come early in the morning. They tie their boats here and ride their bicycles or motorcycles into town. Then in the evening they will come back here, chain their bicycles to the railings over there, and go out in the boats. It is a very old way of life. Every year there are fewer boats here.'

That was sad.

'Where do the people go instead?' Lizhi asked.

Ah Guan made a vague gesture with his hands that included the sea and the rough country surrounding them. 'Even out here the buildings are coming closer. When the environment changes, creatures have to adapt. Come, what would you like to eat?'

There were no cafes or restaurants in sight. A few people were sitting on stools around wooden tables in the shade. As Lizhi and Ah Guan walked past them some people called out greetings to him.

'Is that Mandarin?' Lizhi asked. 'I learned some Mandarin but I couldn't understand what they said.'

'That's Hokkien,' Ah Guan explained, 'and some Cantonese.

If you stay in Singapore longer you will pick it up. Come and sit here.'

Lizhi had gone to restaurants and cafes all over the world with her parents but getting something to eat in Singapore with Ah Guan was different. This was a hawker stall where the night fishermen stopped to get breakfast after a night at sea, Ah Guan told Lizhi.

'What have you got for us today?' Ah Guan shouted after they sat down on wooden stools at a wooden table.

'Sotong balls, otak, pisang goreng, kueh lapis and prawn crackers,' a woman suddenly appeared. 'Why so late today, Uncle?'

Then she saw Lizhi and a big smile appeared on her face. '*Cucu anda? Dia chantik!*'

Ah Guan translated for Lizhi, 'The sotong balls are a very popular fried snack. Often you see people eating them on sticks. Pisang goreng are bananas fried in batter. But for your first real breakfast here we will have fried noodles.'

Though Lizhi wrinkled up her nose at the thought of more noodles, Ah Guan ordered *mee rebus* for them.

'At this time the *nasi lemak* is sold out already. By this time it always is, unless you bring your own fish, then Mak Cik will cook for you. But you cannot come to Singapore and think that the only noodles here are instant noodles!'

Mee rebus turned out to be bright yellow egg noodles in thick gravy. It did not look anything like what Lizhi had been given by Aunt Mona.

'*Mee rebus* means noodles boiled,' explained Ah Guan as the plates were put in front of them. 'Noodles are "mee" and "rebus" means boiled. This is the kind of food you will only get in Singapore. The noodles and mung bean sprouts are Chinese, the spices in the sauce are Malay and the sweet potato bits are Indian. If you like this, one day you should try Indian rojak.'

The gravy tasted of peanuts, which Lizhi loved. There were also sliced hard-boiled eggs, fried shallots, prawn fritters, squid and *hare-bee* which Ah Guan said was dried shrimp. He let Lizhi squeeze the half lime over his plate as well as her own.

It was delicious. Lizhi enjoyed it so much that she even stopped asking questions. Ah Guan and even the stallholders who gathered round their table laughed to see her eating so happily.

'Next time she must come and try the *mee siam*,' one man said to Ah Guan, 'and the *satay*. You must bring her again!'

'But I'm leaving Singapore soon,' Lizhi said with her mouth full.

'Once you eat Singapore food you will always come back,' the man said with assurance. 'Singapore food is like that. It will always bring you back here.'

There was also a coffee for Ah Guan and a cup of Milo for Lizhi. They came with a plate of *kaya* butter toast and four half cooked eggs in a little metal pot standing on a plastic dish.

'You must try—*kaya* toast was your Pa's favourite.'

As soon as she tasted it, Lizhi loved the thick buttery *kaya* toast. As she ate she watched Ah Guan cracking eggs expertly into their dishes. They had soft and cloudy whites with rich orange yolks and Ah Guan added soya sauce and a sprinkle of pepper into the dish before pushing it across the table to Lizhi. It looked interesting but Lizhi hesitated.

'How do you eat this?' she asked.

There was more good-natured laughter in response to this. One of the stall assistants mimed lifting a dish above his lips, then tilting his head backwards and pouring the contents into his mouth. Lizhi was not sure she could manage that.

'Just scoop it into your mouth with the spoon,' Ah Guan suggested. He demonstrated, putting the plate of soft egg to his mouth and swallowing.

Eating directly off plates was one of the things Lizhi had been told that grown-ups never ever did (and that Lizhi herself should never ever do especially when there were adults around) but the rules seemed to be different here. She did as the others had demonstrated. It was a strange sensation; Lizhi felt as though she was swallowing a fluffy cloud that was plump full of warm yellow sunshine.

'Good?'

'Good!' Lizhi said.

'Good. If you eat this every day you will grow strong!'

Lizhi should have been full. But perhaps the memory of instant noodles and the prospect of more instant noodle meals allowed her to eat more than she thought possible. Even after the rich liquid egg was safely in her tummy she managed to finish her kaya toast.

'Your kaya today—not enough pandan taste,' Ah Guan complained to the plump woman who had brought the dish and was now sitting on a stool at the next table watching Lizhi eat. However, it was clear he was not seriously upset. 'And your butter all melted already.'

'How you know?' the woman replied, 'All *habis* already! *Wah*! The small girl can eat, eh?'

'What other Singapore food did your father tell you about?' Ah Guan asked Lizhi.

'He also liked monkey bananas,' Lizhi remembered, 'and blocks of sweet corn and red bean ice cream that you eat out of a folded piece of bread, and mangosteens that are purple outside but white inside and have the same number of segments inside as the pattern on the outside.'

'Next time,' Ah Guan said, 'you will have to stay longer. All these things you can still find here but you need to know where to look. But when you want to go out, you come and find me, okay? No more climbing out of windows!'

'Whose room was the one that I climbed out of?' Lizhi asked. She remembered the drawings and woodcarvings and the little stone mudskipper. She really wanted to show Ah Guan the mudskipper, and even more than that she wanted to take it down to the beach where she could put it close to the real mudskipper holes to see whether they would be taken in by it.

Ah Guan didn't answer her question. 'You cannot mind other people's business like that,' he said. 'There is nothing inside there. Nobody has been inside that room for years!'

Ah Guan said this in the voice that adults use when they mean, 'Don't argue with me because I know I'm right even if I'm wrong'.

Lizhi was cross with Ah Guan. He was either lying to her or he didn't know what he was talking about. Hadn't she seen Aunt Mona in the room taking things out of a drawer? And hadn't she been inside the room herself? She looked at him rebelliously.

'Anyway,' Ah Guan said, 'we must get you back to the house before the tide comes up. And before your auntie starts to worry.'

Even before Lizhi got back to the house she could hear Aunt Mona talking angrily to Bwe Bwe. This was not unusual for Aunt Mona, but Lizhi hoped it would not make Aunt Mona more ready to be cross with her ... since she probably had more reason for that, seeing how muddy she had got.

Lizhi collected her party dress from the tree where it was hanging. Ah Guan helped her get into it. She hoped she would get a chance to wash up before Aunt Mona saw her. The difficulty with washing up in the old house was that you had to tell Bwe Bwe at least an hour ahead of time so that she could switch on the water heater, otherwise you had to wash yourself with cold water. Most of the time Lizhi did not mind this, but after getting doused in mud and seawater she felt it would be good to have some nice hot water to soak it off with.

But Lizhi was unlucky—Aunt Mona must have been waiting for her because no sooner had she got into her room than Aunt Mona came furiously in search of her, with a miserable looking Bwe Bwe trailing behind.

'I was calling and calling for you!' Aunt Mona said. 'I didn't know what had happened to you! I sent Bwe Bwe to find you and she comes back and says, "Don't have." I told her she must be blind! Of course Miss Lizhi must be here somewhere, what do you mean "don't have"!'

From behind Aunt Mona, Bwe Bwe gave Lizhi a small encouraging smile. What was bad luck for Lizhi was actually good luck for Bwe Bwe because now that Aunt Mona had someone else to scold she forgot all about Bwe Bwe.

'Why were you looking for me?' Lizhi asked.

'And what have you been doing?' Aunt Mona finally took in

Lizhi's muddy state and the crumpled remains of the pretty frock that was no longer crisp and white. There was even mud on the pink carnations. Aunt Mona took a deep breath and stared. For a moment Lizhi wondered whether her aunt was going to smack her, she looked so mad. Then Aunt Mona breathed out and said, 'You are a disgrace. Just like your father. You can eat your lunch in the kitchen with Bwe Bwe. I'm not having you in the dining room like that. You'll dirty everything. Bwe Bwe, you better put on the water heater for her.'

It was not as bad as Lizhi had expected. She much preferred eating in the kitchen with Bwe Bwe than sitting at the dining table with Aunt Mona. And Lizhi was so full of the delicious things Ah Guan had bought her that she did not even mind that lunch was instant noodles again.

Lizhi would have liked to tell Bwe Bwe all about her adventures; next time (and Lizhi hoped there would be a next time) she would ask Ah Guan if she could bring back something for Bwe Bwe too. Bwe Bwe did not like instant noodles either.

But she didn't get a chance to talk to Bwe Bwe because Aunt Mona turned up in the kitchen.

Aunt Mona had been so cross with Lizhi that she had forgotten why she had been looking for her.

'Your mother called,' Aunt Mona said. 'She's coming to get you tomorrow morning.'

Lizhi's face lit up. She had had such a good time exploring the mangroves and trying out Ah Guan's Singapore food that she had forgotten to count the hours till her mother's return. 'Goody! Goody! Goody!' Lizhi shouted, bouncing in her chair.

'She's coming back with a man. This Jeremiah fellow,' Aunt Mona said. 'According to her he's some lawyer who's now acting as an agent for her—' Aunt Mona seemed very angry about that.

'Jeremiah is a friend of my Papa,' Lizhi explained. 'And he knows all about how to take care of money and things.'

'So she says,' Aunt Mona said. 'Putting all my brother's things in the hands of some total stranger. It's obvious, isn't it, what she's up to?'

'What?' wondered Lizhi, who didn't find it obvious at all.

Something was on Aunt Mona's mind. Lizhi could see from the way she fidgeted that she was trying to decide how to put what she had to say.

'You wait and see. That mother of yours is going to marry this man and he's going to swindle her and take all the money for your father's paintings. You just wait and see. Why else would some stranger suddenly get so chummy with someone like her? So tall and so black!'

'Jeremiah is Papa's friend,' Lizhi pointed out. 'He's just trying to help Mama.'

'Supposedly. If he's really interested in that mother of yours you know what's going to happen? They're going to abandon you, dump you here in Singapore for us to look after. Why would a young woman like that want to be stuck with a child?'

'Did Mama say that to you over the phone?' Lizhi did not believe it. She wanted to call and talk to her mother right away, but Aunt Mona said, 'It's your fault for not being around when your mother phoned. Now that she can see that you are too busy running around to talk to her, she can go off and have a good time and not worry about you being here.'

'I want to phone her,' Lizhi said again.

'I'm surprised she stuck with your father for so long, if you ask me. If not for you she would probably have left long ago. But she couldn't leave you with someone as irresponsible as your father ...'

'And now she's getting her hooks into another Chinese man! It's disgusting the way she operates. Even seeing what comes out of mixing different kinds of people!' When Aunt Mona said that she looked at Lizhi with the same look on her face as when she told Bwe Bwe that the floor was still dirty.

'It must have been such a difficult life for him, you know. Always wandering from one location to another, always packing and repacking and trying to get enough work to keep that woman happy ... and having to support a child as well. Must have been a great responsibility for him.'

Lizhi felt guilty. After all she was the child Aunt Mona was talking about. She had been partly responsible for how tired her father had been. And perhaps if he had not been so tired and worried about her all the time he would have seen the car coming and not been killed in the accident after all. Then Lizhi would not be in Singapore now being scolded by Aunt Mona.

Lizhi looked at Aunt Mona and saw with some surprise that she was enjoying herself. 'You are a bully,' Lizhi told her. 'And you are a liar too!'

Whether or not Lizhi was right did not make any difference. Aunt Mona might be a bully but she was also a grown-up in charge of the house and Lizhi got sent to her room for daring to talk back.

'You can stay in there until you learn to have some respect for your elders!' Aunt Mona said as she locked the door to Lizhi's room. 'And I'm going to tell your mother all about your behaviour—if she can take enough time away from that man of hers to remember she has a daughter!' There was no more mention of the bath Lizhi was supposed to have and Aunt Mona did not say what time her mother would be arriving the next day.

Lizhi was dirty, upset and angry. She decided that she was already in so much trouble it would not make much difference what she did. She might be locked into her room but her previous window escape had taught her there was more than one way to get in and out of rooms in that house.

Lizhi did not really mean to be naughty or to steal. She just really wanted to see the carved mudskipper again and she wanted to go to the beach once more before she left Singapore forever. It seemed like a very good idea to take the little stone mudskipper to the beach to compare it to the other mudskippers there.

And if Aunt Mona thought she was locked in her room it was the perfect time to pay a last visit.

Lizhi managed to climb out of her bedroom window and edge along the outside ledge before climbing into the locked room. It was lucky, she thought, that the hooks on the old window shutters had all fallen off. Lizhi found the mudskipper in its little green bag and made her exit. All the climbing and jumping was making her tired. Lizhi decided she did not want to be a burglar after all.

'Miss! Miss!' Lizhi saw Bwe Bwe carrying the rubbish bags out to the bin along the main road. 'If you run away Mam will be very angry with you! She will scold you very much!' Bwe Bwe said. 'Much better you wait until your mother come tomorrow, then at least you can go home!'

'I'll come back before tomorrow,' Lizhi said. 'I'm just going to look at the mudskippers one last time.' She made Bwe Bwe promise not to tell anyone.

'Everybody now got secrets,' Bwe Bwe said. 'Old man also got secrets. I cannot remember everything.'

'You mean the gardener? What secrets?' Lizhi wanted to know. But Bwe Bwe wouldn't tell and Lizhi set off on her own. It was already late afternoon and would be evening soon but Lizhi was confident she knew the way. She wanted to find the muddy beach where they had seen the mudskippers and hermit crabs.

Though Lizhi did not admit it even to herself, she wanted to get away from Aunt Mona's house and the things she had said about her parents. Lizhi figured that if she could just stay away from Aunt Mona until her mother came to collect her she need never think about the things her aunt had said again. And then things could go back to how they used to be.

Except of course, things would never be completely the same again because her father would still be dead and her mother might still marry someone else and leave her in Aunt Mona's house forever.

It was more difficult getting across the mangrove swamp alone. Without Ah Guan there the swamp seemed darker and the roots and branches more tangled, but Lizhi ploughed on, clutching her precious brown stone mudskipper in its little cloth bag. She looped the string to tie the bag around her wrist so she would not drop it.

Finally she made it to the big rock and managed to climb

around and across it even though the rocks she had to step on were all under water now. But when she finally got across there were no mudskippers on the beach. In fact there was hardly any beach left. The tide had come up over the stones and was pushing its way right up the beach. The waves were dark and forceful, almost angry, as they threw themselves onto the sand and rocks, forcing themselves higher and higher up and pushing Lizhi down till she could not help but fall. Lizhi was all wet now. To make it worse it was starting to rain, the wind rattling the trees and making whistling, shrieking sounds in the trees. She still held tight onto her precious mudskipper in its wet cloth bag. Lizhi felt scared.

SAFE IN THE SWAMP

Then strong arms were picking her up and lifting her out of the water. Lizhi saw that it was Ah Guan who had found her. The old man lifted her easily and set her on one of the higher rocks so that only her legs were still in the pounding sea. However tall Ah Guan might have been, the angry waves still came up above his waist, throwing him against the rocks as he stood there holding Lizhi.

'Are you all right?'

'Yes.' Lizhi had never been so glad to see anyone before, but she knew she deserved to be scolded for sneaking out. Ah Guan hauled himself up onto the rocky ledge beside Lizhi.

'We must go up higher,' was all the old man said. 'The sea is still rising.'

Ah Guan made Lizhi climb onto his back and hold on tight. Even though she had only met him that morning Lizhi instinctively felt safe with him. Not since her father died had she trusted anyone so completely. Step by step Ah Guan climbed out of reach of the rising sea and up onto the rocky ledge where Lizhi had seen the little shrine earlier. The ledge had seemed so high up that morning, but now the waves almost reached it. It was still raining, and the rain water rushing down into the sea clashed with the water crashing upwards from the rising tide.

'The water won't come up beyond that dark line on the rock.' Ah Guan saw Lizhi watching the level of the water.

'Even when it's raining?'

'Even when it's raining.'

The rain was getting heavier and there was not much shelter except from the trees growing on the sheer slope above them. But the wind had died down and the rain came down in big warm drops.

‘What are you doing here?’ Lizhi asked Ah Guan before he could ask her.

‘Bwe Bwe told me you came out,’ Ah Guan said.

‘How are we going to get back?’

‘We wait.’

‘But what if Aunt Mona—’

‘We have to wait,’ Ah Guan said. ‘No choice.’

The rain stopped and the storm clouds shifted so the sky was no longer as dark as it had been. The sea was no longer rising because the tide had turned and even the waves lapped gently against the rocks they had crashed against so furiously before.

‘What about these marks?’ Lizhi asked, pointing to the rock face behind them. ‘There are lines here too. Does the water ever come up this high?’

‘Not since the tsunami,’ Ah Guan said. ‘These are marks made by iron deposits. It’s the same in the rock all the way down, but we can only see it where it has broken off.’

They spent that night on the rocks. Lizhi decided that even if Aunt Mona was angry, sometimes it was better to stay where you knew it was safe instead of trying to get back because people might be worrying.

‘Are you scared?’ Lizhi asked Ah Guan in a small voice. ‘Should we try to escape?’

'The sea will go down and the sun will rise,' Ah Guan said, 'and we are safe here until then. But we must wait for the right time to go home.'

That was true. 'But what if we miss the right time and the sea comes up again?' Lizhi asked. 'My father always said he would come home to Singapore when the right time came but he never did.'

Ah Guan did not answer. Then, just as Lizhi was falling asleep, he asked, 'Why did you say you hate your grandfather?'

Lizhi didn't know. She had only said what she felt because of what she had heard from her parents. Even though Ah Guan was being even more inquisitive than Aunt Mona, Lizhi wasn't angry with him.

'I suppose because of my father—'

'Why did your father hate your grandfather?'

After all, there was nothing wrong with asking questions because you wanted to find out things. Lizhi herself asked questions all the time. What she didn't like was people who pretended to ask questions but were really trying to make you think in a particular way. That was what Aunt Mona had been doing, Lizhi saw now. But there was no point getting upset with Aunt Mona either. Aunt Mona might rage like the rain and the waves but eventually she had to stop.

'I don't think my father really hated my grandfather,' Lizhi said. 'I know he blamed himself for not introducing my mama to his parents properly and giving them time to get to know each other better. He said somehow they got off on the wrong foot and never made up. That's why first impressions are so important. But he always said he wished his parents could have seen me so I don't think he was really angry with them.'

Ah Guan frowned. 'I'm sure your grandparents wanted to see you too,' he said. 'They would have sent you cards and letters on your birthday and for Christmas they would have sent presents. That's the kind of thing grandparents do, even when they are angry—no?'

Lizhi shook her head. That was the kind of thing her French grandparents did. They were always sending toys, sweets, sausages and impractical presents like battery-run chickens that laid chocolate eggs, whenever they were not in the same country for Christmas or birthdays or name days. Lizhi knew very well the difference between grandparents who did and did not send things.

'No they didn't. I would have seen them. I always collected our mail with Mama because of the stamps—in some hotels they would let me have stamps that other guests didn't want. Anyway, my grandmother is dead after being sick for a long time and my grandfather is sick now so they couldn't have sent anything.'

'They could have asked somebody to post it for them,' Ah Guan said stubbornly. 'I'm sure they weren't living alone.

They could have asked someone to mail the things for them.'

Lizhi thought of Aunt Mona. 'They could have but they didn't. Papa's sister who lives with them is the one who told Papa that her parents never forgave Mama and him and we shouldn't visit them because they were still so angry. And now, even though I am in Singapore, she says my grandfather went to stay in the hospital not just because he's sick but because he doesn't want to see me.'

Ah Guan shook his head as though not believing Lizhi.

'Like when I was born. Papa wrote to his parents to ask them to choose a Chinese name for me. But they never answered, and Papa had to call Aunt Mona who said they didn't want anything to do with his mixed-race child.'

Ah Guan stared out into the sea. He was so still that Lizhi did not know if he had heard her. When he finally spoke again he said, 'Do you think about your father a lot?'

'I'm afraid to,' Lizhi admitted. 'Because it makes me feel sad and I want to be strong for Mama. But I'm also afraid of forgetting him.'

Ah Guan looked so sad that Lizhi felt sorry. Then she remembered she had something that might make him feel better—and also prove to him that she had been right all along about the locked room.

‘Can you keep a secret?’ Lizhi asked the old man.

‘Depends.’

‘You can’t say depends. You have to swear. Cross your heart and hope to die, poke a needle in your eye.’

The old man looked dubious. Lizhi decided to trust him anyway.

‘Look.’ She took the looped bag off her wrist and pulled the little stone mudskipper out of its pouch and held it up to show him.

‘It’s a secret, because it’s not really mine. But I’m looking after it for a while because I’m showing it what the sea is like.’

The old man’s response was entirely satisfactory. He stared, then reached out and took it gently. ‘He got it then. And you brought it back with you. After all these years.’

Lizhi didn’t know what he was talking about.

‘I have to get it back to the house before Aunt Mona misses it,’ she told the old man. ‘So that I can put it back in Aunt Mona’s room. It’s the room that you saw me climbing out of, that you said nobody ever goes into. I just borrowed it to play with for a while so I didn’t ask her, but it’s not really stealing.’

‘Are you sure?’ the old man asked, turning the tiny statue over in his hands. ‘Are you sure that’s where you found it?’

‘Of course!’ Lizhi said. ‘If you promise not to tell anyone I’ll show you. It was in a cupboard in the room with all of Aunt

Mona's papers. But—are you allowed inside the house?' Lizhi was not sure exactly where a gardener was supposed to spend his time.

For a moment the old man looked as though he was going to say something angrily, but instead he just said, 'I'll figure something out.'

That suited Lizhi.

Almost without realising it, Lizhi fell asleep. She dreamed she was sitting on her father's lap with his arms around her, keeping her safe and warm. She could almost hear her father talking about the sea. How clear the warm waters were long ago when they first moved into the house by the sea—so clear that you could see not only the fish swimming but even the coral on the seabed. 'All things change,' the calm steady voice said. You have to change with them in order to remain steady. In her dream, Lizhi could not tell the difference between her father and Ah Guan.

NEXT MORNING

It was early morning when Lizhi awoke. The sky was all light blue with golden streaks, the clouds were huge and pinkish white, and best of all, the tide had gone down. Now, with the pale blue sky blending into the peaceful, barely darker blue grey sea, it seemed incredible that there could have been anything frightening about this place the night before.

Lizhi could see where the tide pools had been left by the receding tide. The small creatures in them were as lost in the dry air and daylight as she had been in the darkness and water. The grass was wet with dew and so were her underpants and the back of her dress, but that was all right.

Ah Guan was sitting on a rock, watching her. Lizhi wondered whether he had been watching her all night. She was wet and dirty and sore from sleeping curled up on the ledge and she had grazed her knees when she had slipped on the slippery rocks in the dark.

'I have to go back now,' she said. Lizhi knew she would be in trouble with Aunt Mona and her mother too, if she had already arrived. But even if her mother was angry with her (and though she had felt so angry with her mother after listening to what Aunt Mona said), Lizhi suddenly felt she couldn't wait to see her.

'Drink something first.' Ah Guan had collected some water for them to drink.

Some birds swooped by. They were having a wonderful time in the shallow water, and on the damp grass of the slopes above, pecking at grubs dislodged by the rain. Some of them had got a light green fruit off a tree and were squabbling over it.

'Can humans eat that?' Lizhi asked, realising she was hungry. The birds seemed to love eating the fruit.

'No. It's a cacao tree. People make chocolate from the fruit but we can't eat it as it is. Not without some treatment. Not everything suits everybody.'

'The tide is turning. It will be going down soon,' Ah Guan said. 'And then it will be safe to go back.'

Lizhi had not realised till she moved how thirsty and stiff

she was. But she was so excited about getting back and seeing her mother it did not matter.

Though the tide was going down and they could see most of the rocks it was not yet low tide. The water came up to Lizhi's knees and thighs as Ah Guan helped her make her way over the rocks, but in the morning sun it was calm and almost warm. Now as gentle little waves swirled around her Lizhi remembered how frightening the sea had been the night before and shivered.

'Here,' Ah Guan said. 'Slowly, slowly. Do you want to wait until it goes down further?'

'Oh no, oh no. Let's go now. My mama may be there already and I don't want her to worry.'

'Better she is angry with you for going back late than sad because you never get back.'

Lizhi said, 'And then there's Jeremiah.' She twisted her face as she said the name 'Jeremiah'. Suddenly Lizhi felt that she hated Jeremiah more than she had ever hated anyone before in her life. 'I hate Jeremiah,' she said.

'Who is Jeremiah?'

'He was a friend of my father,' Lizhi said. 'And he went to China to help my mother talk to people about my father's paintings and now he's here in Singapore.' Lizhi could see that Ah Guan was going to ask more questions, so very quickly she added, 'I don't want to talk about him.'

'Why?' Ah Guan asked.

'I just don't, that's all.'

Ah Guan looked at Lizhi thoughtfully. 'Okay. And why don't you like this Jeremiah?'

Lizhi exhaled noisily. 'Isn't it obvious?' she demanded. She was not sure why it should be obvious, but it had been to Aunt Mona. 'It's just how things are!' she added.

'What's this Uncle Jeremiah like?' Ah Guan asked again as they started walking through the swamp on the far side of the rock crossing. The roof of the house was visible now.

'Look, I said I don't want to talk about him.'

'If you don't like him, I don't like him either. But I need to be able to recognise him,' Ah Guan pointed out.

That made sense. Lizhi tried to describe Uncle Jeremiah. 'He's Chinese, like my father. He's a lawyer.'

'Why do you hate him so much?'

'Because if he marries my mama he will want to go away with her and they will leave me to be a burden on Aunt Mona.'

'But if he marries your mother he may want to be your father, right?'

'It won't be the same thing at all!' Lizhi said. 'We won't be a real family. It will all be a fake, a bluff, a con!'

She felt angry with Ah Guan because he did not seem to grasp something that was so obvious to her. 'You can't just get married and become a family instantly. That's not a real family. It's artificial!'

'Just because something is artificial does not mean it is not real. These mangrove swamps are artificial. But the trees in them are real. The life in here is real. Even if a family is artificial it doesn't mean it's not real.'

'A mangrove swamp is different,' Lizhi said. 'Trees don't care where they grow anyway.'

They reached Ah Guan's hut at the old breakwater, and he stopped walking. Lizhi stood on one leg and then the other, not sure whether to ask him to go up to the house with her. She could not see any sign of her mother or a taxi, and it seemed much pleasanter to remain outside, next to the mangrove, than return to the mustiness of the cluttered house.

'Do you know mangrove trees deliberately send their seeds far away so that their shadows will not prevent them from sprouting? If the sprouting seeds root too close to the parent tree the new plant will be weak because it won't get enough sun. So the mangroves wait till the tide is right and the seedlings are ready and they let the tide take the young plants far away where they can find their own space and put down their roots and grow.'

'Do you think my mother is sending me away from her?' Lizhi said, alarmed.

'No tree would send a seed away until it is ready to float and sprout,' Ah Guan said. 'If you tear it away before it is ready it may die. But another big problem is some trees get so tangled up trying to protect their offspring that they wind their roots around them to keep them safe. But that might actually kill the young plant so it has to break away if that happens, even if it means tearing away a part of the parent plant.'

Ah Guan was talking to himself more than to Lizhi.

IN TROUBLE WITH AUNT MONA AGAIN

Ah Guan started to walk with Lizhi to the house, but then he disappeared once they heard angry, excited voices coming from the veranda. Lizhi was cross for a moment because Ah Guan could have told them that he had been with her all night and she had been safe all along. But then, maybe, he was afraid of being fired.

Lizhi's mother and Jeremiah had just arrived and there was a big furore going on, mainly because Juliette had just learned that not only was Lizhi missing but Aunt Mona had not even realised she wasn't there.

At the same time Aunt Mona was trying to make a fuss about Juliette not having given her their flight details and just turning up in the house without warning her (though they had told her they were coming they had not told her exactly when). But it was clear that Lizhi's mother's fuss was much bigger and noisier.

Jeremiah saw Lizhi before the women did. While they shouted at each other and shouted for Lizhi, Jeremiah had been walking up and down, scanning the garden and the swamps beyond, so he was the first to call out, 'There she is!' Lizhi's mother let out a loud shriek and ran across the wet lawn to Lizhi, not stopping even when her high-heeled sandals fell off.

Juliette put her arms around Lizhi and squeezed her so hard it was impossible to understand how she could see Lizhi as a problem or want to get rid of her.

'I am so so so angry with you!' she said, in between laughing and crying. Jeremiah was laughing and crying too. Then he took both Lizhi and her mother into his arms and squeezed them both, and Lizhi could feel him shaking.

'I called the police,' Jeremiah said, 'and the coast guard. And the army, because they have boats in the area. I should let them know you're all right. Oh my god, if anything happened to you—'

'A lot of fuss about nothing,' Aunt Mona said. 'They will probably fine you for making a false report. This is the second time the girl ran off. She is stubborn and sneaky and rude!' Her mother, busy kissing Lizhi and saying how angry she was with her precious darling baby girl, didn't pay any attention.

'She is safe,' Jeremiah said. 'That is all that matters.'

As he spoke, with one arm around Lizhi's shoulders, Lizhi recognised and remembered the real Uncle Jeremiah. This was Uncle Jeremiah, her father's best friend, who loved both Lizhi and her mother. He was not the monster that Aunt Mona had created. It was too easy to believe what people made up and get so angry you refused to see how things were for yourself.

Aunt Mona was watching them with a grim expression.

'So is the happy reunion finished?' Aunt Mona said. 'She needs some strict discipline, this girl. She is rude and totally unmanageable.'

'Aunt Mona is worried that you're going to marry Mama to get Papa's paintings and money,' Lizhi told Jeremiah. 'And that you're going to leave me here with her because you don't want to be bothered with me.' Lizhi was not telling tales. She thought that if Uncle Jeremiah could explain to Aunt Mona they had no intention of dumping Lizhi on her then Aunt Mona would not be so worried and cross all the time.

Jeremiah stopped to text a message on his mobile before he spoke. Then he put his arm back around Lizhi's shoulders and said, 'If that is how you feel, I will take full responsibility for Lizhi's financial future, for Michael's sake.'

Then Juliette and Aunt Mona both started shouting at him and at each other again. Lizhi thought they were all being silly and childish. She was hungry and thirsty and the mud drying on her made her feel cold and sticky, but the adults seemed to have forgotten that she was there.

'Papa didn't like people to shout at each other,' Lizhi said.

'Will you shut up about your Papa? Your stupid Papa is dead,' said Aunt Mona loudly, 'and I'm sick of hearing about what he wanted or didn't want!'

Lizhi's mother made a strange sound. It was halfway between a groan and a sob and there were tears running down her face. Lizhi was suddenly very angry, though she still didn't know what was happening. She threw her arms around her mother's waist to protect her and shouted at Aunt Mona, 'I hate you! I hate you and my horrible grandfather too! I don't care if he doesn't want to see me—I don't want to see him either! You are all horrible and don't deserve to be related to my Papa who was a genius and a wonderful man, and if you don't shut up I will kick you!'

Lizhi had never spoken like that to a grown-up before. She clenched her hands into little fists, not because she was going to hit or kick anybody but because it seemed like the right thing to do when you were very angry.

To her surprise Aunt Mona seemed almost pleased. She looked at the other two and said, 'You see how she behaves? No manners at all and no respect for her elders.'

'How do you think she should treat her elders?' Ah Guan said. He had come up around the house so quietly that none of them saw him till he spoke.

Aunt Mona's mouth shaped into a round 'O' of shock. Then she hissed, 'Not now! They're still here; are you blind?'

'He's the gardener,' Lizhi whispered to her mother and Jeremiah. 'He saved my life.' But they were staring at the old man and didn't pay any attention to her.

'I showed her some of my favourite places in the mangroves,' the old man said. 'They were some of her father's favourite places too. You crowded the house too full of bad memories, that's why I couldn't stay in the house after your Ma died.'

'I've been to Michael's room,' the old man continued. 'The locked room—that you said you were keeping exactly as it was until he came back.' He was talking to Aunt Mona. 'I found the letters from your brother and his wife, and the photos of Lizhi they sent. I also found my own letters to them—the letters my wife wrote to them—never posted.'

Aunt Mona was looking ill. 'I was only protecting you,' she whispered. 'These people only want to swindle you ...'

'Mona, the problem with you is that you never throw out anything,' Ah Guan said. 'You fill up the house with useless rubbish. But the good thing is that you didn't throw out the valuable things either.'

Aunt Mona stood opening and closing her mouth. Then she pointed a finger at Lizhi, 'It's all her fault!' she said. 'Everything was fine until she came!'

'She's just like her father,' the old man said. He spoke softly, and Lizhi could not tell whether he thought this was a good thing or a bad thing. He looked at her mother and held up several sheets of writing paper.

'My son writes here that his Juliette looks like a fairytale princess come to life. See here? "My Juliette is tall and beautiful and has long brown hair and big shining eyes, and she glows because she is always smiling or laughing. I know you will love her as much as I do when you meet her."'

Juliette tried to say something but she choked on the words.

'Thank you for making my son happy,' Ah Guan said.

'Are you my grandfather then?' Lizhi asked the old man. 'Why didn't you tell me? I thought you were the gardener! And you know all about the plants and the animals in the mangrove swamp, just like Papa! Mama, he showed me a real mudskipper!' Lizhi had already forgotten the grown-ups' argument. Now that she remembered it the mudskipper was far more important. 'And it was just like Papa said it was. Not a fish and not a frog but in between!'

But the old man—Lizhi's grandfather—was not finished with her yet.

'Why did you say that you hated your grandfather?' he asked her.

'Oh, that was before I knew it was you,' Lizhi said honestly. 'I already like you. But my grandfather—' Lizhi remembered the things she had been told about her grandfather and looked at the old man with her head tilted to one side so that she could study him better. To the adults she looked like a puppy trying to decide whether or not the stranger holding out a treat could be trusted. She decided he could be.

'Well, I only hated you because you hated me first,' Lizhi explained. 'I knew all about Papa fighting with you because you didn't want him to marry Mama. And then after Papa died and Mama wanted to bring me to meet you because she promised Papa she would, you didn't want to see me.'

Lizhi's grandfather looked at her mother. 'I promised Michael that I would bring her to see you,' Lizhi's mother said. 'It was the last, most important thing. Not because we need your money or anything.'

Aunt Mona snorted and said, 'As if,' but no one paid any attention to her.

Lizhi's Mother said softly, 'I'm sorry I took so long to bring her back, Mr Wang.' 'No, Juliette,' said the old man. 'I'm sorry. And you don't call me Mr Wang, you call me Apa, okay?'

Even Lizhi had understood by then that Aunt Mona had been hiding the letters that her parents wrote to her grandparents, and also the letters and presents and money that her grandparents had given her to post to them. Aunt Mona had told her grandfather that her parents were too proud to ask for forgiveness just as she had told Lizhi's father that his parents were still too angry to want to see him again.

'Mona, how could you?' Lizhi's grandfather asked.

'After all I've done for you—you are just a selfish, stubborn, wicked old man! Even now you can't see these people are only after your money!'

'I did know about Michael's mother wanting to leave the house to Lizhi,' Juliette said. 'But we didn't—that is, Michael didn't hold her to it. It was enough for us to know that she wanted to do that for her granddaughter. He was so upset that you informed him about her death only after the funeral.'

'You're lying,' Aunt Mona sneered desperately. 'There's no way you could know anything about that. Nobody knew but me, and I made sure she never sent you anything!'

'I'm not so sure,' Grandfather said. He looked at Bwe Bwe who was hiding behind Aunt Mona. Bwe Bwe looked even smaller and more miserable than before. 'Did you post anything for Aunty Granny?'

'Please Sir,' Bwe Bwe said. 'Don't ask me!'

Aunt Mona stared at her.

'You did, didn't you?' Grandfather said.

'Please Sir, Aunty Granny give me money to send things back for my family and also to send to her son. She put on the address and I go and walk to the postman and give him money for the stamp and take back to post.'

'Did you show her these drawings?'

He was holding some drawings that looked like her father's sketches of Lizhi when she was a baby and just learning to walk. Bwe Bwe nodded miserably.

'I'm going to send you home!' Aunt Mona said furiously to Bwe Bwe. 'I'm not going to give you any money and I'm going to tell the people at your agency that you are always lying and stealing things. You will never get another job in Singapore! You will never be able to pay back the money that your family borrowed to send you here. Your family will all starve and it will be your fault!'

'No,' said Grandfather.

'If you want me to run your house you must let me run it my way!' Aunt Mona said.

'I don't want you to run my house,' Lizhi's grandfather said.

Aunt Mona seemed to crumble as she stood there. Lizhi felt almost sorry for her as Bwe Bwe helped her gently back into the house.

HAPPY ENDING

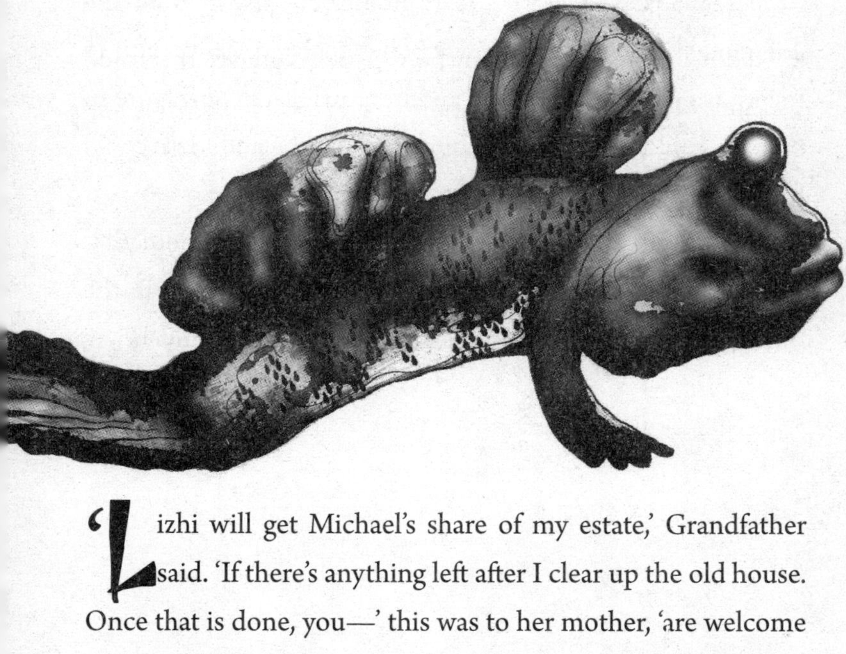

'Lizhi will get Michael's share of my estate,' Grandfather said. 'If there's anything left after I clear up the old house. Once that is done, you—' this was to her mother, 'are welcome to consider this your home whenever you want. I always meant to divide everything between my two children, and Mona has already taken more than her share.'

The old house was much more comfortable after her grandfather let Bwe Bwe clean out the closed rooms. He moved back into the main house and there was always a bedroom ready for Lizhi when she wanted to spend her holidays there.

Aunt Mona moved to a flat in the city. She asked Bwe Bwe to go with her but Bwe Bwe preferred to stay in the big house by the sea because she had got used to it and she liked looking after Lizhi's grandfather who never shouted at her.

Jeremiah did not marry Lizhi's mother, but thanks to him she got enough money from the sale of her husband's last paintings to buy a small flat in Paris and another small flat in Singapore so that she could work in both countries, and she and Lizhi could travel back and forth.

And every time Lizhi visited Singapore, her grandfather would take her to the mangrove swamps to look at the mudskippers that his son and her father had loved so much.